HELLO GORGEOUS!

I see that you are a smart, determined gogetter ready to create your joyous life. Thank you for the amazing company. With your **JOY MANIFESTO**, you are literally going to design the exact future of your dreams. This mindset success tool will help you increase your **JOY** and cultivate daily habits that will create massive amounts of happiness and abundance. I know you are ready so let's go!

HOW TO USE YOUR JOY MANIFESTO:

The first 5 pages lays the foundation for your future. Filling these out is essential to get laser focused on what your **DREAM** life will look like. This also trains your brain to "see" all the good in your life right **NOW**.

VISUALIZING: Life changing tool that rewires your brain to take action and achieve your dreams.

PURPOSE: Honor your top priorities when making all decisions, it keeps life simple.

WORDS: Powerful brain "treats" to think positive. Repeat your affirmations daily.

GRATITUDE: Cultivating this creates even more of what you are grateful for.

GOAL SETTING: Essential for clarity and creation of what brings you joy and fulfillment.

For 90 days you will have 2 pages per each day to fill out with reminders for a **HAPPY, HEALTHY, PURPOSE DRIVEN, JOYFUL LIFE.** Fill out the top left page each morning, and complete the bottom each evening. Use the right hand side to plan your day and stay on track. Pick your top 3 daily goals that will bring your 10 yearly goals to fruition.

MEDITATION: Lifts the fog of thoughts to increase your creativity and give you peace.

HEALTH: Take care of your body so you can be the best joyful, energized YOU.

FUN: Savoring what life has to offer. You cannot be all work and no play or you'll burn out...do something fun every day!

GIVING: This is what life is all about. It can be a phone call, a message, a smile or something tangible.

CELEBRATION: Essential and deserved...go ahead and pat yourself on the back.

Every 30 days you'll take a "coffee break" to reevaluate your goals and progress.

I cannot wait to hear the incredible accomplishments the next 90 days brings you. Please, share your story with me on my website or on social media!

With love,
Gretchen

L'ART DE VIVRE!

the art of living

VISUALIZE A DAY IN YOUR DREAM LIFE AND WRITE IT HERE.
DREAM BIG. MONEY IS NO OBJECT.

who would be with you? how do you **FEEL**?
what do you see? what do you hear?

be **SPECIFIC!**

RAISON D'ÊTRE! WHAT ARE YOUR TOP 2-3 PRIORITIES (FAMILY, HEALTH, CAREER, FAITH ETC)? WRITE HERE. WHEN MAKING DECISIONS ASK YOURSELF *"does this honor my top priorities?"* IF NOT.....POLITELY DECLINE.

PAIN AU CHOCOLAT FOR YOUR BRAIN!

WRITE YOUR TOP MANTRAS AND AFFIRMATIONS HERE!

EX: *"every day and every way i'm getting better and better. i am happy, i am healthy."*

LA VIE EST BELLE!

"life is beautiful"

GRATITUDE. BRAIN DUMP EVERYTHING YOU ARE GRATEFUL FOR

be SPECIFIC!

VIVRE LA VIE PAR LA CONCEPTION!

living a life by design. create your joyful life!

WRITE YOUR 10 GOALS FOR THE NEXT 1 YEAR HERE. WHAT WILL BRING YOU JOY ??

1.
2.
3.
4.
5.
6.
7.
8.
9.
10.

GOOD MORNING gorgeous!

I AM GRATEFUL FOR

FUN!!! TODAY FOR FUN I WILL

- [ ] **VISUALIZATION** – SET YOUR TIMER FOR A MINIMUM OF 5 MINUTES AND GO THERE!
- [ ] **MEDITATION** – SET YOUR TIMER FOR A MINIMUM OF 5 MINUTES AND BE PRESENT, IN THE NOW. BREATHE.
- [ ] **EXERCISE** – DID YOU MOVE AT LEAST 30 MINUTES TODAY?
- [ ] **FUEL** – EAT 80% NUTRIENT DENSE FOOD THAT ENERGIZES YOU

I WAS MOST GRATEFUL FOR TODAY

Good Evening Gorgeous!

I LOVE TO GIVE. TODAY I GAVE

CHEERS TO ME!!!
LET'S CELEBRATE MY SUCCESSES FOR THE DAY

I AM BRILLIANT
gorgeous
TALENTED AND FABULOUS

GOOD MORNING gorgeous!

I AM GRATEFUL FOR
....
....
....

MY MANTRA for today!
....
....
....
....

FUN!!! TODAY FOR FUN I WILL
....
....
....

- ☐ **VISUALIZATION** – SET YOUR TIMER FOR A MINIMUM OF 5 MINUTES AND GO THERE!
- ☐ **MEDITATION** – SET YOUR TIMER FOR A MINIMUM OF 5 MINUTES AND BE PRESENT, IN THE NOW. BREATHE.
- ☐ **EXERCISE** – DID YOU MOVE AT LEAST 30 MINUTES TODAY?
- ☐ **FUEL** – EAT 80% NUTRIENT DENSE FOOD THAT ENERGIZES YOU

I WAS MOST GRATEFUL FOR TODAY
....
....
....
....
....

Good Evening Gorgeous!

I LOVE TO GIVE. TODAY I GAVE
....
....
....

CHEERS TO ME!!!
LET'S CELEBRATE MY SUCCESSES FOR THE DAY
....
....
....

I AM BRILLIANT
gorgeous
TALENTED AND FABULOUS

GOOD MORNING *gorgeous!*

I AM GRATEFUL FOR

MY MANTRA *for today!*

FUN!!! TODAY FOR FUN I WILL

- [ ] **VISUALIZATION** – SET YOUR TIMER FOR A MINIMUM OF 5 MINUTES AND GO THERE!
- [ ] **MEDITATION** – SET YOUR TIMER FOR A MINIMUM OF 5 MINUTES AND BE PRESENT, IN THE NOW. BREATHE.
- [ ] **EXERCISE** – DID YOU MOVE AT LEAST 30 MINUTES TODAY?
- [ ] **FUEL** – EAT 80% NUTRIENT DENSE FOOD THAT ENERGIZES YOU

I WAS MOST GRATEFUL FOR TODAY

Good Evening Gorgeous!

I LOVE TO GIVE. TODAY I GAVE

CHEERS TO ME!!!
LET'S CELEBRATE MY SUCCESSES FOR THE DAY

I AM BRILLIANT
gorgeous
TALENTED AND FABULOUS

GOOD MORNING gorgeous!

I AM GRATEFUL FOR

FUN!!! TODAY FOR FUN I WILL

- ☐ VISUALIZATION – SET YOUR TIMER FOR A MINIMUM OF 5 MINUTES AND GO THERE!
- ☐ MEDITATION – SET YOUR TIMER FOR A MINIMUM OF 5 MINUTES AND BE PRESENT, IN THE NOW. BREATHE.
- ☐ EXERCISE – DID YOU MOVE AT LEAST 30 MINUTES TODAY?
- ☐ FUEL – EAT 80% NUTRIENT DENSE FOOD THAT ENERGIZES YOU

I WAS MOST GRATEFUL FOR TODAY

Good Evening Gorgeous!

I LOVE TO GIVE. TODAY I GAVE

CHEERS TO ME!!!
LET'S CELEBRATE MY SUCCESSES FOR THE DAY

I AM BRILLIANT
gorgeous
TALENTED AND FABULOUS

GOOD MORNING *gorgeous!*

MY MANTRA *for today!*

_____
_____
_____
_____

I AM GRATEFUL FOR
_____
_____
_____

FUN!!! TODAY FOR FUN I WILL
_____
_____
_____

- ☐ **VISUALIZATION** – SET YOUR TIMER FOR A MINIMUM OF 5 MINUTES AND GO THERE!
- ☐ **MEDITATION** – SET YOUR TIMER FOR A MINIMUM OF 5 MINUTES AND BE PRESENT, IN THE NOW. BREATHE.
- ☐ **EXERCISE** – DID YOU MOVE AT LEAST 30 MINUTES TODAY?
- ☐ **FUEL** – EAT 80% NUTRIENT DENSE FOOD THAT ENERGIZES YOU

I WAS MOST GRATEFUL FOR TODAY
_____
_____
_____
_____
_____
_____

Good Evening Gorgeous!

I LOVE TO GIVE. TODAY I GAVE
_____
_____
_____

CHEERS TO ME!!!
LET'S CELEBRATE MY SUCCESSES FOR THE DAY
_____
_____
_____

I AM BRILLIANT
gorgeous
TALENTED AND FABULOUS

GOOD MORNING *gorgeous!*

I AM GRATEFUL FOR
_____
_____
_____
_____

MY MANTRA

for today!
_____
_____
_____

FUN!!! TODAY FOR FUN I WILL
_____
_____
_____

☐ VISUALIZATION – SET YOUR TIMER FOR A MINIMUM OF 5 MINUTES AND GO THERE!

☐ MEDITATION – SET YOUR TIMER FOR A MINIMUM OF 5 MINUTES AND BE PRESENT, IN THE NOW. BREATHE.

☐ EXERCISE – DID YOU MOVE AT LEAST 30 MINUTES TODAY?

☐ FUEL – EAT 80% NUTRIENT DENSE FOOD THAT ENERGIZES YOU

I WAS MOST GRATEFUL FOR TODAY
_____
_____
_____
_____
_____

Good Evening Gorgeous!

I LOVE TO GIVE. TODAY I GAVE
_____
_____
_____

CHEERS TO ME!!!
LET'S CELEBRATE MY SUCCESSES FOR THE DAY
_____
_____
_____

I AM BRILLIANT
gorgeous
TALENTED AND FABULOUS

GOOD MORNING gorgeous!

I AM GRATEFUL FOR

FUN!!! TODAY FOR FUN I WILL

- ☐ **VISUALIZATION** – SET YOUR TIMER FOR A MINIMUM OF 5 MINUTES AND GO THERE!
- ☐ **MEDITATION** – SET YOUR TIMER FOR A MINIMUM OF 5 MINUTES AND BE PRESENT, IN THE NOW. BREATHE.
- ☐ **EXERCISE** – DID YOU MOVE AT LEAST 30 MINUTES TODAY?
- ☐ **FUEL** – EAT 80% NUTRIENT DENSE FOOD THAT ENERGIZES YOU

I WAS MOST GRATEFUL FOR TODAY

Good Evening Gorgeous!

I LOVE TO GIVE. TODAY I GAVE

CHEERS TO ME!!!
LET'S CELEBRATE MY SUCCESSES FOR THE DAY

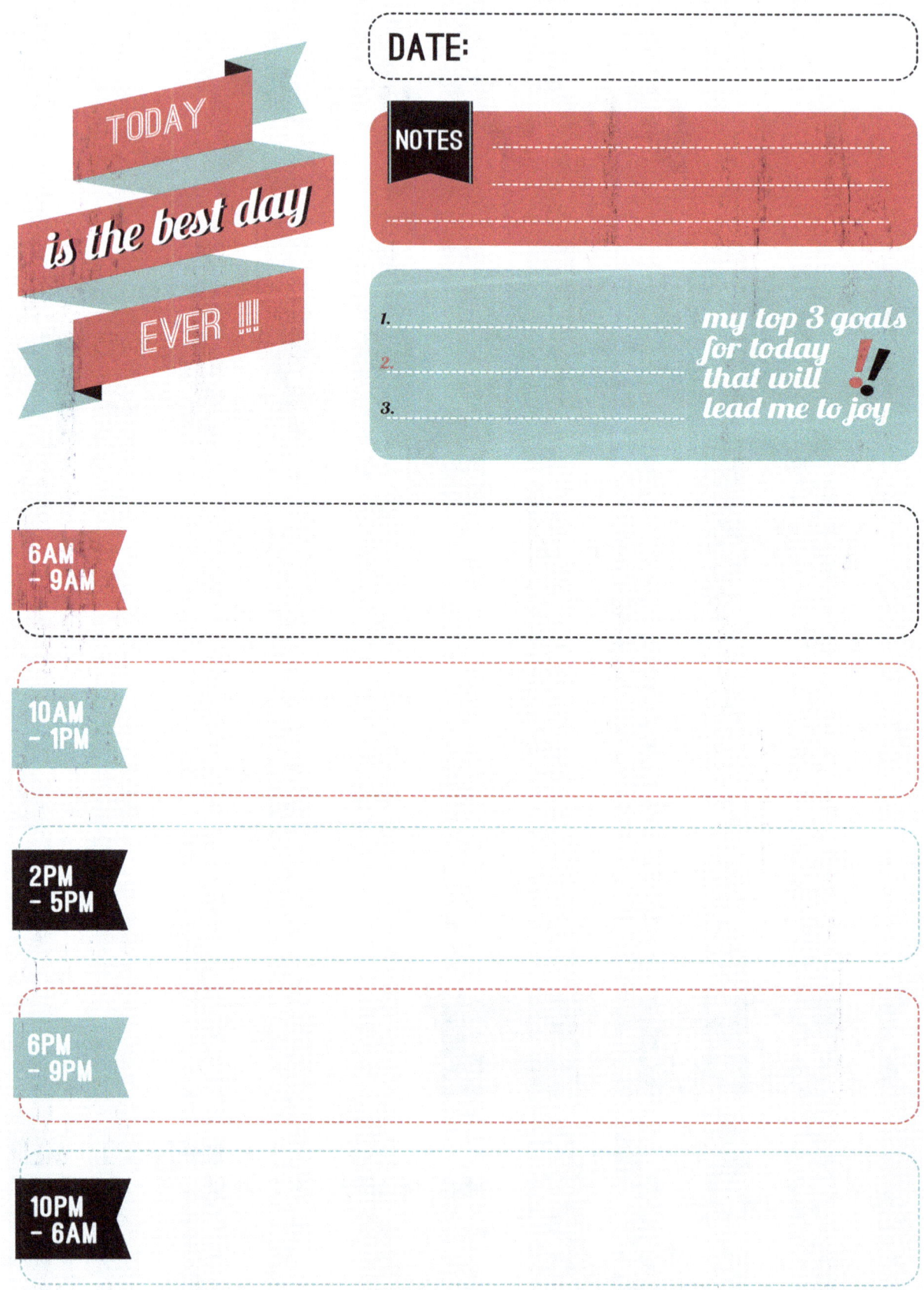

I AM BRILLIANT
gorgeous
TALENTED AND FABULOUS

GOOD MORNING *gorgeous!*

I AM GRATEFUL FOR
_____
_____
_____

MY MANTRA *for today!*
_____
_____
_____
_____

FUN!!! TODAY FOR FUN I WILL
_____
_____
_____

- ☐ **VISUALIZATION** – SET YOUR TIMER FOR A MINIMUM OF 5 MINUTES AND GO THERE!
- ☐ **MEDITATION** – SET YOUR TIMER FOR A MINIMUM OF 5 MINUTES AND BE PRESENT. IN THE NOW. BREATHE.
- ☐ **EXERCISE** – DID YOU MOVE AT LEAST 30 MINUTES TODAY?
- ☐ **FUEL** – EAT 80% NUTRIENT DENSE FOOD THAT ENERGIZES YOU

I WAS MOST GRATEFUL FOR TODAY
_____
_____
_____
_____
_____

Good Evening Gorgeous!

I LOVE TO GIVE. TODAY I GAVE
_____
_____
_____

CHEERS TO ME!!!
LET'S CELEBRATE MY SUCCESSES FOR THE DAY
_____
_____
_____

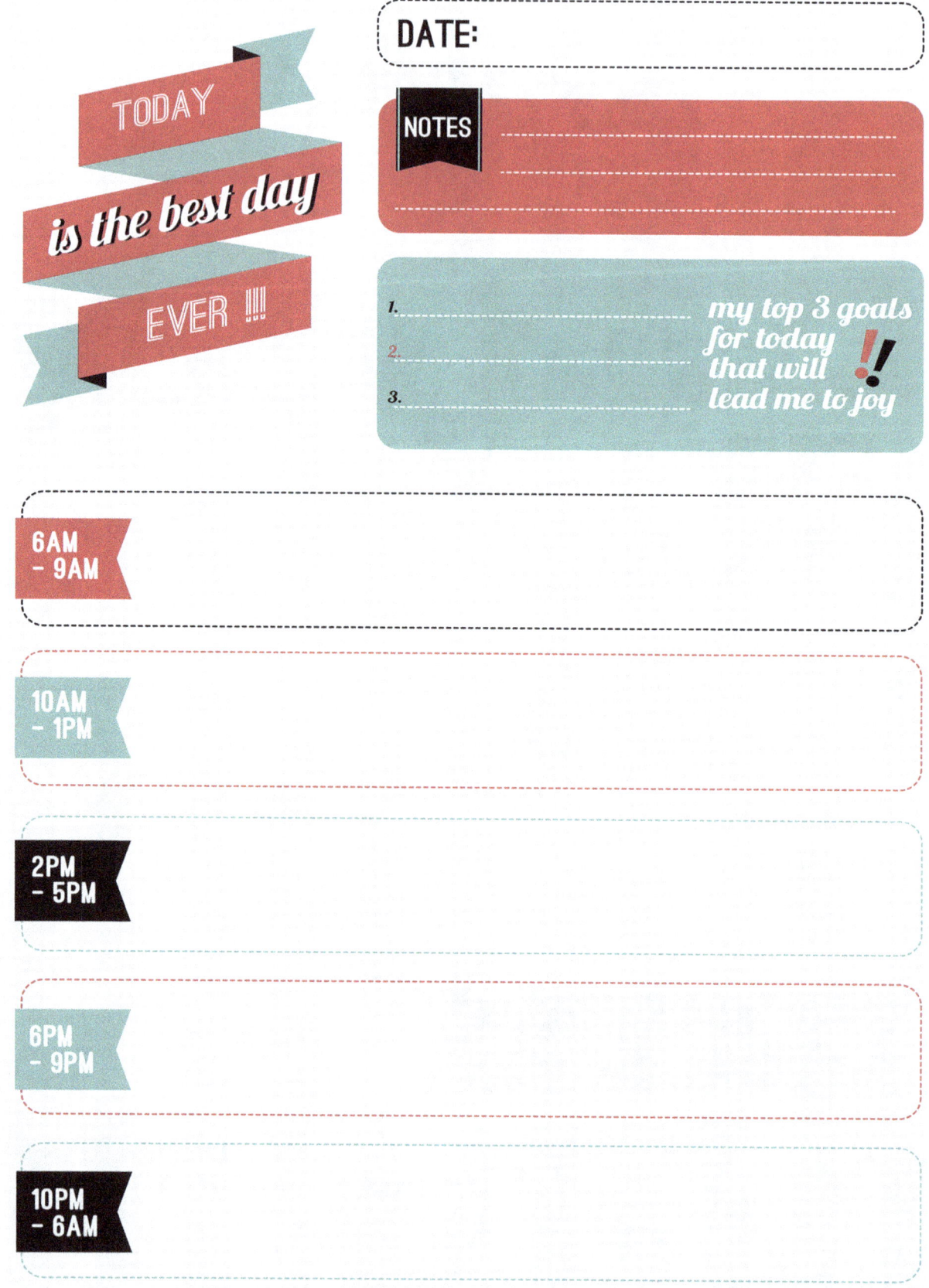

I AM BRILLIANT
gorgeous
TALENTED AND FABULOUS

GOOD MORNING gorgeous!

I AM GRATEFUL FOR

....
....
....
....

MY MANTRA for today!

....
....
....
....

FUN!!! TODAY FOR FUN I WILL

....
....
....

- ☐ **VISUALIZATION** – SET YOUR TIMER FOR A MINIMUM OF 5 MINUTES AND GO THERE!
- ☐ **MEDITATION** – SET YOUR TIMER FOR A MINIMUM OF 5 MINUTES AND BE PRESENT, IN THE NOW. BREATHE.
- ☐ **EXERCISE** – DID YOU MOVE AT LEAST 30 MINUTES TODAY?
- ☐ **FUEL** – EAT 80% NUTRIENT DENSE FOOD THAT ENERGIZES YOU

I WAS MOST GRATEFUL FOR TODAY

....
....
....
....
....
....
....

Good Evening Gorgeous!

I LOVE TO GIVE. TODAY I GAVE

....
....
....

CHEERS TO ME!!!
LET'S CELEBRATE MY SUCCESSES FOR THE DAY

....
....
....

I AM BRILLIANT
gorgeous
TALENTED AND FABULOUS

GOOD MORNING gorgeous!

I AM GRATEFUL FOR

MY MANTRA *for today!*

FUN!!! TODAY FOR FUN I WILL

☐ **VISUALIZATION** - SET YOUR TIMER FOR A MINIMUM OF 5 MINUTES AND GO THERE!

☐ **MEDITATION** - SET YOUR TIMER FOR A MINIMUM OF 5 MINUTES AND BE PRESENT, IN THE NOW. BREATHE.

☐ **EXERCISE** - DID YOU MOVE AT LEAST 30 MINUTES TODAY?

☐ **FUEL** - EAT 80% NUTRIENT DENSE FOOD THAT ENERGIZES YOU

I WAS MOST GRATEFUL FOR TODAY

Good Evening Gorgeous!

I LOVE TO GIVE. TODAY I GAVE

CHEERS TO ME!!!
LET'S CELEBRATE MY SUCCESSES FOR THE DAY

GOOD MORNING gorgeous!

I AM GRATEFUL FOR
....
....
....
....

MY MANTRA for today!
....
....
....
....

FUN!!! TODAY FOR FUN I WILL
....
....
....

- ☐ **VISUALIZATION** – SET YOUR TIMER FOR A MINIMUM OF 5 MINUTES AND GO THERE!
- ☐ **MEDITATION** – SET YOUR TIMER FOR A MINIMUM OF 5 MINUTES AND BE PRESENT, IN THE NOW. BREATHE.
- ☐ **EXERCISE** – DID YOU MOVE AT LEAST 30 MINUTES TODAY?
- ☐ **FUEL** – EAT 80% NUTRIENT DENSE FOOD THAT ENERGIZES YOU

I WAS MOST GRATEFUL FOR TODAY
....
....
....
....
....
....

Good Evening Gorgeous!

I LOVE TO GIVE. TODAY I GAVE
....
....
....

CHEERS TO ME!!!
LET'S CELEBRATE MY SUCCESSES FOR THE DAY
....
....
....

I AM BRILLIANT
gorgeous
TALENTED AND FABULOUS

GOOD MORNING *gorgeous!*

I AM GRATEFUL FOR
_____
_____
_____

MY MANTRA for today!
_____
_____
_____
_____

FUN!!! TODAY FOR FUN I WILL
_____
_____
_____

- ☐ **VISUALIZATION** – SET YOUR TIMER FOR A MINIMUM OF 5 MINUTES AND GO THERE!
- ☐ **MEDITATION** – SET YOUR TIMER FOR A MINIMUM OF 5 MINUTES AND BE PRESENT, IN THE NOW. BREATHE.
- ☐ **EXERCISE** – DID YOU MOVE AT LEAST 30 MINUTES TODAY?
- ☐ **FUEL** – EAT 80% NUTRIENT DENSE FOOD THAT ENERGIZES YOU

I WAS MOST GRATEFUL FOR TODAY
_____
_____
_____
_____
_____

Good Evening Gorgeous!

I LOVE TO GIVE. TODAY I GAVE
_____
_____
_____

CHEERS TO ME!!!
LET'S CELEBRATE MY SUCCESSES FOR THE DAY
_____
_____
_____

DATE:

NOTES

1. ....
2. ....
3. ....

my top 3 goals for today that will lead me to joy !!

6AM – 9AM

10AM – 1PM

2PM – 5PM

6PM – 9PM

10PM – 6AM

make sure you get your sleep!

I AM BRILLIANT
gorgeous
TALENTED AND FABULOUS

GOOD MORNING gorgeous!

I AM GRATEFUL FOR

MY MANTRA for today!

FUN!!! TODAY FOR FUN I WILL

- ☐ **VISUALIZATION** – SET YOUR TIMER FOR A MINIMUM OF 5 MINUTES AND GO THERE!
- ☐ **MEDITATION** – SET YOUR TIMER FOR A MINIMUM OF 5 MINUTES AND BE PRESENT, IN THE NOW. BREATHE.
- ☐ **EXERCISE** – DID YOU MOVE AT LEAST 30 MINUTES TODAY?
- ☐ **FUEL** – EAT 80% NUTRIENT DENSE FOOD THAT ENERGIZES YOU

I WAS MOST GRATEFUL FOR TODAY

Good Evening Gorgeous!

I LOVE TO GIVE. TODAY I GAVE

CHEERS TO ME!!!
LET'S CELEBRATE MY SUCCESSES FOR THE DAY

DATE:

NOTES

1. _____
2. _____
3. _____

my top 3 goals for today that will lead me to joy !!

TODAY is the best day EVER !!!

6AM – 9AM

10AM – 1PM

2PM – 5PM

6PM – 9PM

10PM – 6AM

make sure you get your sleep!

I AM BRILLIANT
gorgeous
TALENTED AND FABULOUS

GOOD MORNING gorgeous!

I AM GRATEFUL FOR

MY MANTRA *for today!*

FUN!!! TODAY FOR FUN I WILL

- ☐ VISUALIZATION – SET YOUR TIMER FOR A MINIMUM OF 5 MINUTES AND GO THERE!
- ☐ MEDITATION – SET YOUR TIMER FOR A MINIMUM OF 5 MINUTES AND BE PRESENT, IN THE NOW. BREATHE.
- ☐ EXERCISE – DID YOU MOVE AT LEAST 30 MINUTES TODAY?
- ☐ FUEL – EAT 80% NUTRIENT DENSE FOOD THAT ENERGIZES YOU

I WAS MOST GRATEFUL FOR TODAY

Good Evening Gorgeous!

I LOVE TO GIVE. TODAY I GAVE

CHEERS TO ME!!!
LET'S CELEBRATE MY SUCCESSES FOR THE DAY

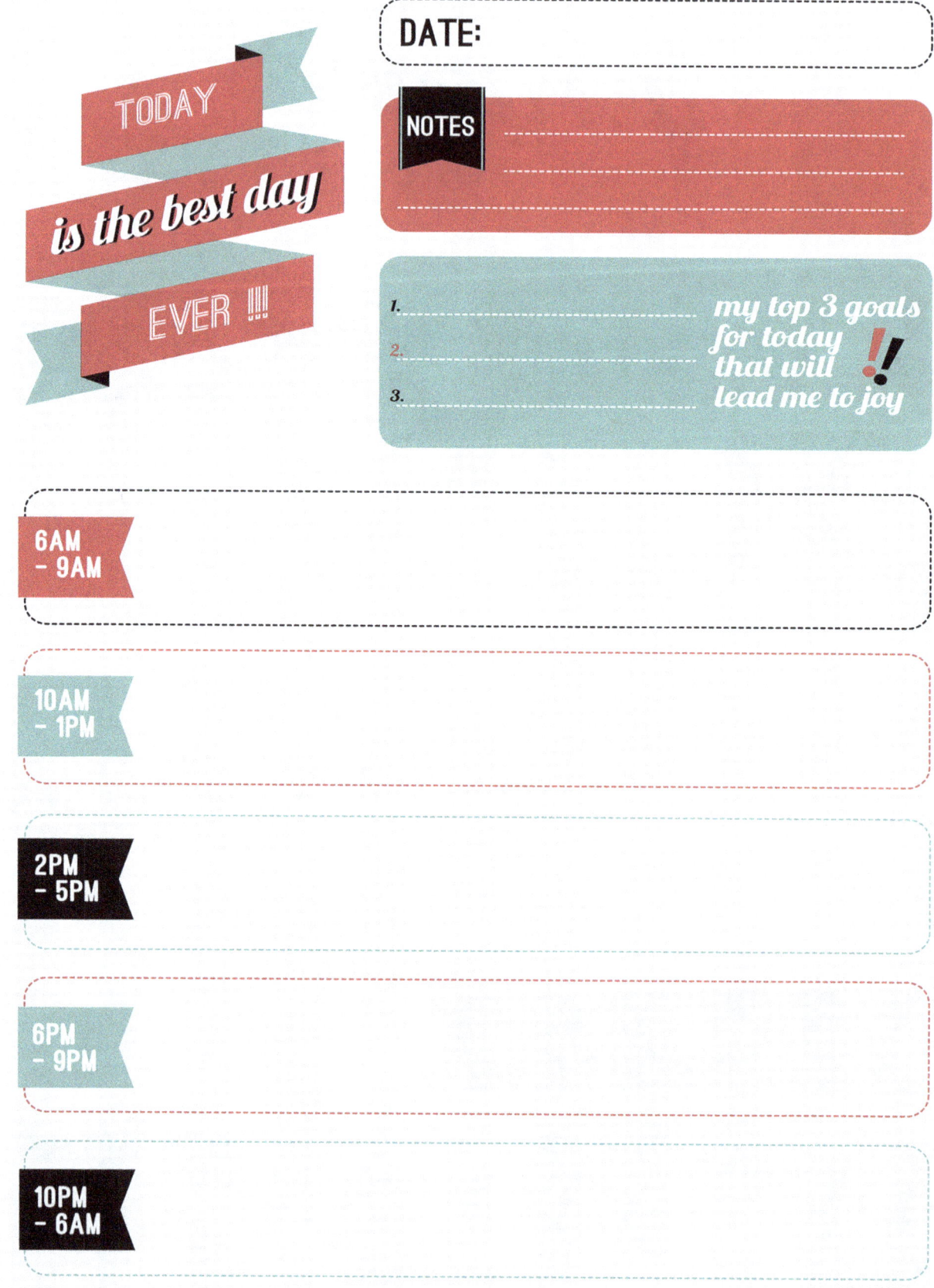

I AM BRILLIANT
gorgeous
TALENTED AND FABULOUS

GOOD MORNING gorgeous!

I AM GRATEFUL FOR

MY MANTRA for today!

FUN!!! TODAY FOR FUN I WILL

- ☐ **VISUALIZATION** – SET YOUR TIMER FOR A MINIMUM OF 5 MINUTES AND GO THERE!
- ☐ **MEDITATION** – SET YOUR TIMER FOR A MINIMUM OF 5 MINUTES AND BE PRESENT, IN THE NOW. BREATHE.
- ☐ **EXERCISE** – DID YOU MOVE AT LEAST 30 MINUTES TODAY?
- ☐ **FUEL** – EAT 80% NUTRIENT DENSE FOOD THAT ENERGIZES YOU

I WAS MOST GRATEFUL FOR TODAY

Good Evening Gorgeous!

I LOVE TO GIVE. TODAY I GAVE

CHEERS TO ME!!!
LET'S CELEBRATE MY SUCCESSES FOR THE DAY

I AM BRILLIANT
gorgeous
TALENTED AND FABULOUS

GOOD MORNING gorgeous!

I AM GRATEFUL FOR

MY MANTRA

FUN!!! TODAY FOR FUN I WILL

☐ **VISUALIZATION** – SET YOUR TIMER FOR A MINIMUM OF 5 MINUTES AND GO THERE!
☐ **MEDITATION** – SET YOUR TIMER FOR A MINIMUM OF 5 MINUTES AND BE PRESENT, IN THE NOW. BREATHE.
☐ **EXERCISE** – DID YOU MOVE AT LEAST 30 MINUTES TODAY?
☐ **FUEL** – EAT 80% NUTRIENT DENSE FOOD THAT ENERGIZES YOU

I WAS MOST GRATEFUL FOR TODAY

Good Evening Gorgeous!

I LOVE TO GIVE. TODAY I GAVE

CHEERS TO ME!!!
LET'S CELEBRATE MY SUCCESSES FOR THE DAY

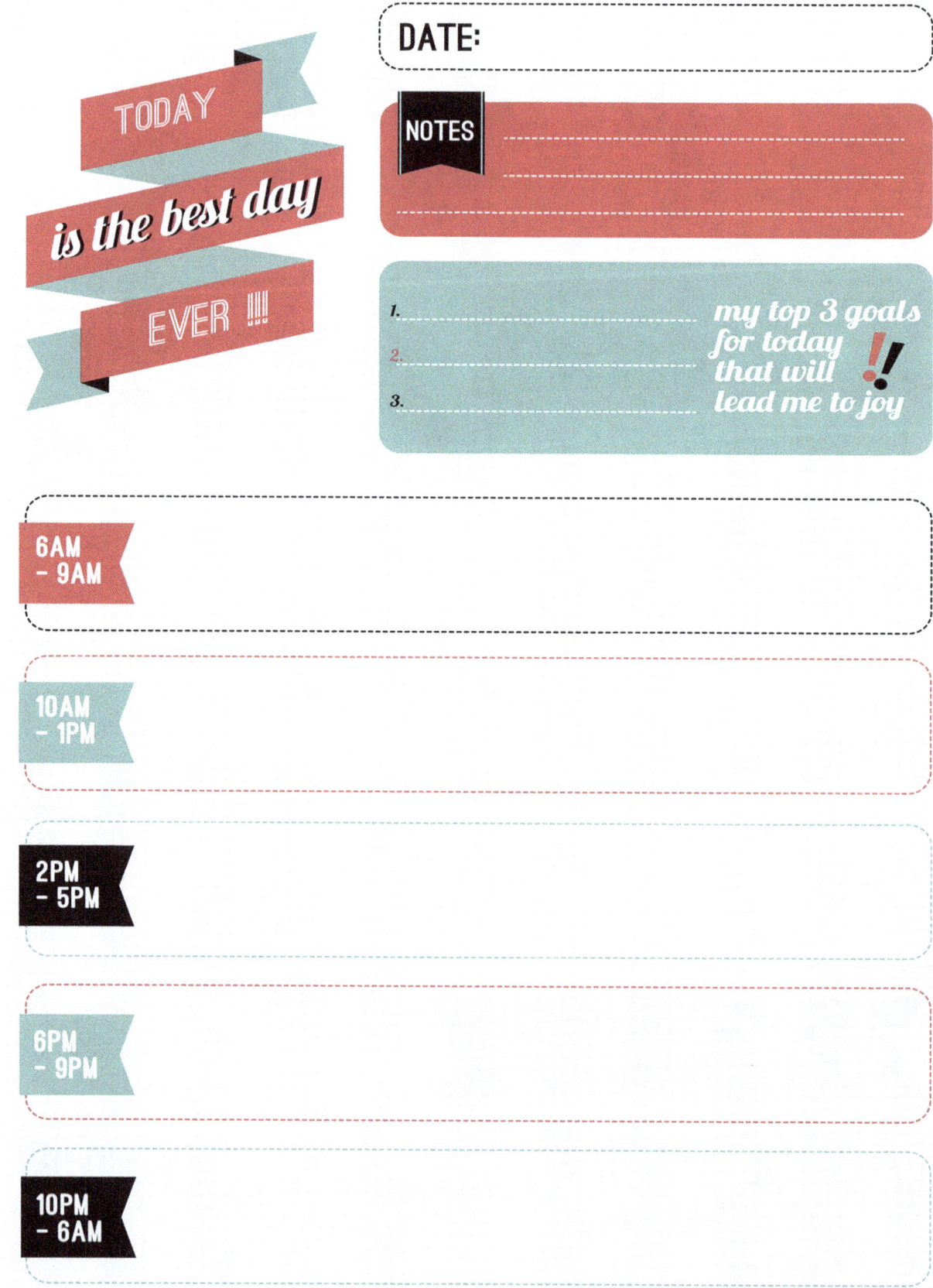

I AM BRILLIANT
gorgeous
TALENTED AND FABULOUS

GOOD MORNING gorgeous!

I AM GRATEFUL FOR

MY MANTRA *for today!*

FUN!!! TODAY FOR FUN I WILL

- [ ] VISUALIZATION – SET YOUR TIMER FOR A MINIMUM OF 5 MINUTES AND GO THERE!
- [ ] MEDITATION – SET YOUR TIMER FOR A MINIMUM OF 5 MINUTES AND BE PRESENT, IN THE NOW. BREATHE.
- [ ] EXERCISE – DID YOU MOVE AT LEAST 30 MINUTES TODAY?
- [ ] FUEL – EAT 80% NUTRIENT DENSE FOOD THAT ENERGIZES YOU

I WAS MOST GRATEFUL FOR TODAY

Good Evening Gorgeous!

I LOVE TO GIVE. TODAY I GAVE

CHEERS TO ME!!!
LET'S CELEBRATE MY SUCCESSES FOR THE DAY

GOOD MORNING gorgeous!

I AM GRATEFUL FOR

MY MANTRA for today!

FUN!!! TODAY FOR FUN I WILL

- ☐ **VISUALIZATION** – SET YOUR TIMER FOR A MINIMUM OF 5 MINUTES AND GO THERE!
- ☐ **MEDITATION** – SET YOUR TIMER FOR A MINIMUM OF 5 MINUTES AND BE PRESENT, IN THE NOW. BREATHE.
- ☐ **EXERCISE** – DID YOU MOVE AT LEAST 30 MINUTES TODAY?
- ☐ **FUEL** – EAT 80% NUTRIENT DENSE FOOD THAT ENERGIZES YOU

I WAS MOST GRATEFUL FOR TODAY

Good Evening Gorgeous!

I LOVE TO GIVE. TODAY I GAVE

CHEERS TO ME!!!
LET'S CELEBRATE MY SUCCESSES FOR THE DAY

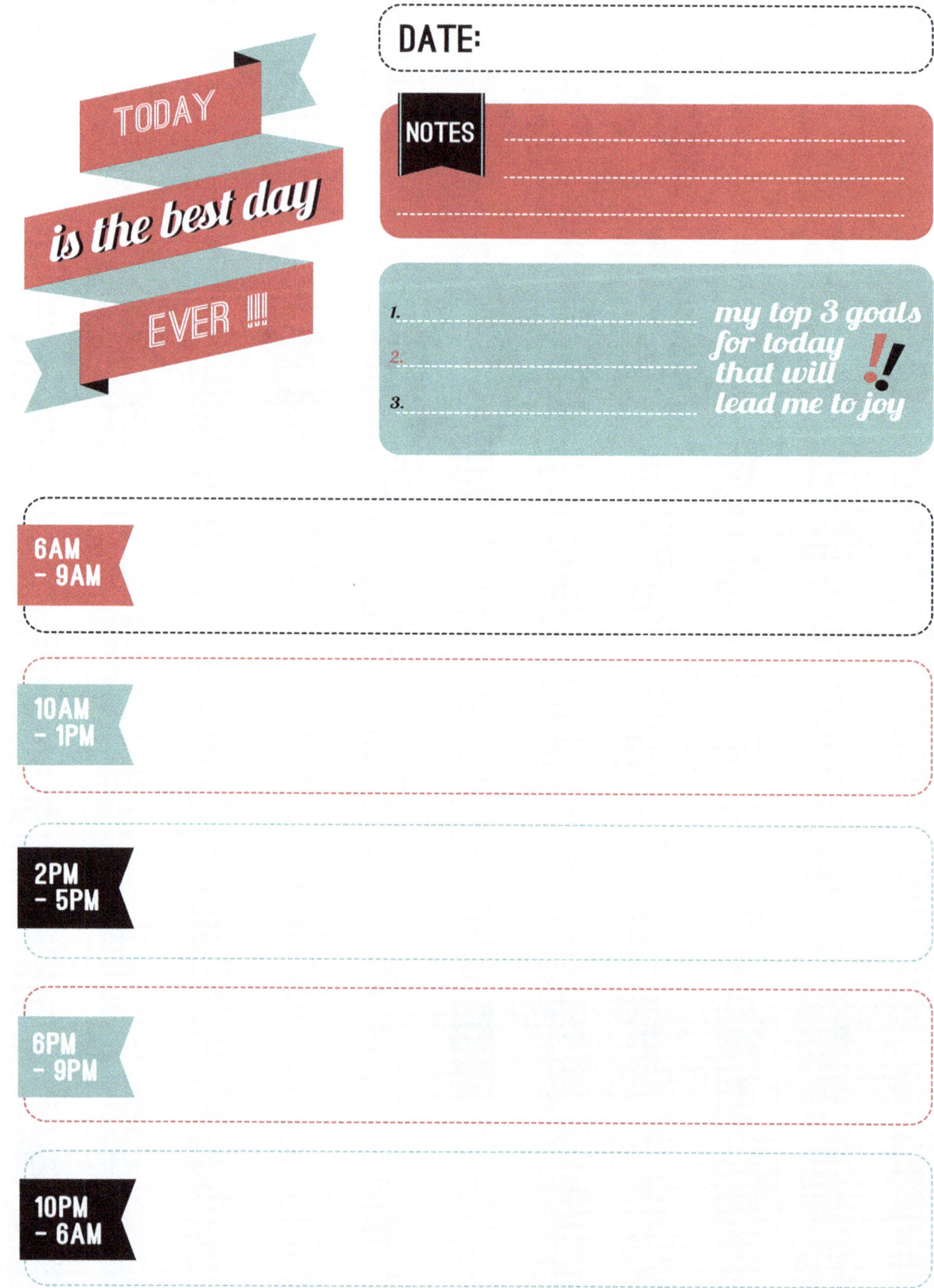

I AM BRILLIANT
gorgeous
TALENTED AND FABULOUS

GOOD MORNING gorgeous!

I AM GRATEFUL FOR

MY MANTRA *for today!*

FUN!!! TODAY FOR FUN I WILL

☐ **VISUALIZATION** – SET YOUR TIMER FOR A MINIMUM OF 5 MINUTES AND GO THERE!

☐ **MEDITATION** – SET YOUR TIMER FOR A MINIMUM OF 5 MINUTES AND BE PRESENT, IN THE NOW. BREATHE.

☐ **EXERCISE** – DID YOU MOVE AT LEAST 30 MINUTES TODAY?

☐ **FUEL** – EAT 80% NUTRIENT DENSE FOOD THAT ENERGIZES YOU

I WAS MOST GRATEFUL FOR TODAY

Good Evening Gorgeous!

I LOVE TO GIVE. TODAY I GAVE

CHEERS TO ME!!!
LET'S CELEBRATE MY SUCCESSES FOR THE DAY

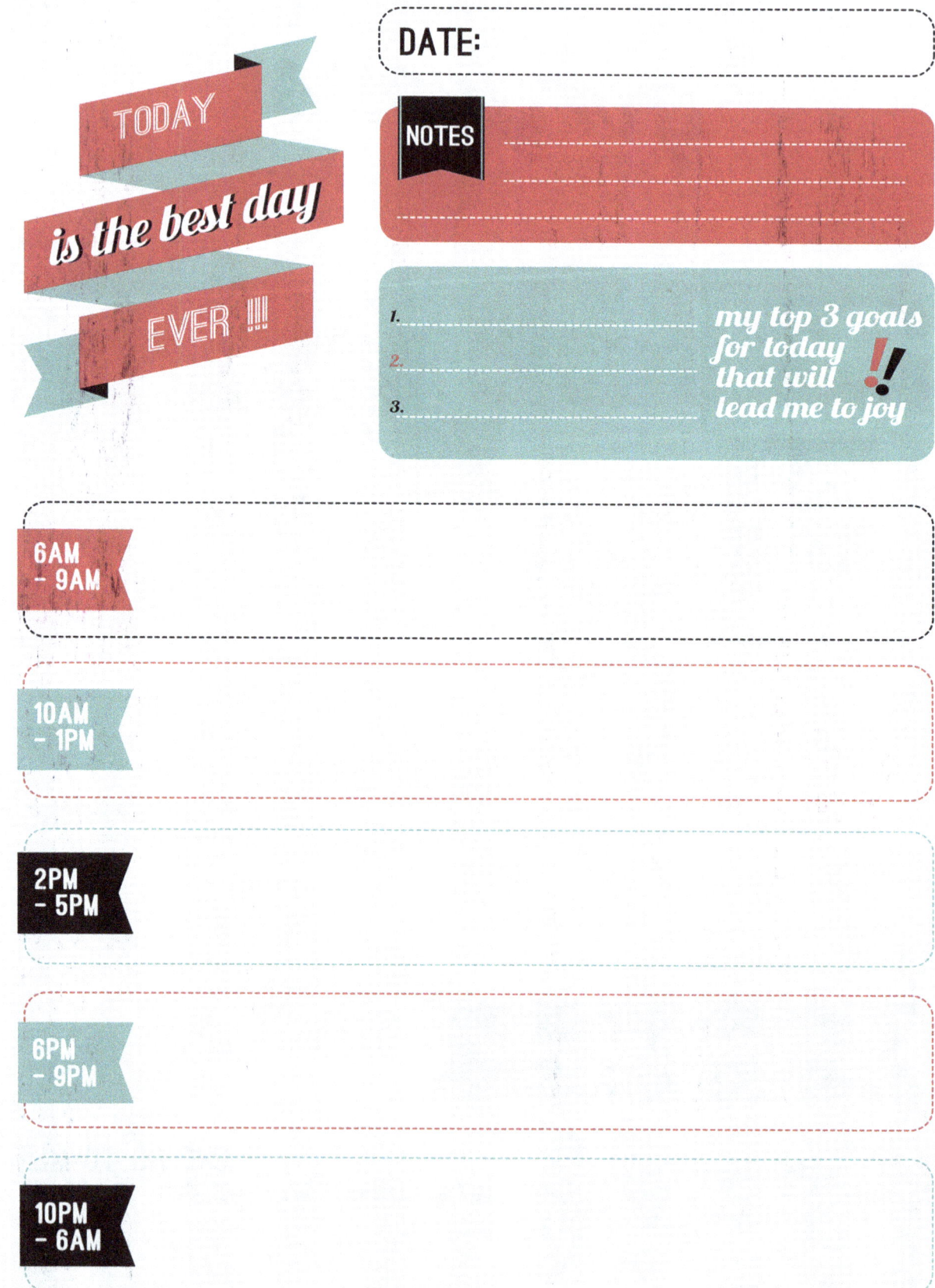

I AM BRILLIANT
gorgeous
TALENTED AND FABULOUS

GOOD MORNING gorgeous!

I AM GRATEFUL FOR
....
....
....

MY MANTRA
....
....
....
....

FUN!!! TODAY FOR FUN I WILL
....
....
....

- ☐ **VISUALIZATION** – SET YOUR TIMER FOR A MINIMUM OF 5 MINUTES AND GO THERE!
- ☐ **MEDITATION** – SET YOUR TIMER FOR A MINIMUM OF 5 MINUTES AND BE PRESENT, IN THE NOW. BREATHE.
- ☐ **EXERCISE** – DID YOU MOVE AT LEAST 30 MINUTES TODAY?
- ☐ **FUEL** – EAT 80% NUTRIENT DENSE FOOD THAT ENERGIZES YOU

I WAS MOST GRATEFUL FOR TODAY
....
....
....
....
....

Good Evening Gorgeous!

I LOVE TO GIVE. TODAY I GAVE
....
....
....
....

CHEERS TO ME!!!
LET'S CELEBRATE MY SUCCESSES FOR THE DAY
....
....
....
....

I AM BRILLIANT
gorgeous
TALENTED AND FABULOUS

GOOD MORNING gorgeous!

I AM GRATEFUL FOR

MY MANTRA for today!

FUN!!! TODAY FOR FUN I WILL

- [ ] **VISUALIZATION** – SET YOUR TIMER FOR A MINIMUM OF 5 MINUTES AND GO THERE!
- [ ] **MEDITATION** – SET YOUR TIMER FOR A MINIMUM OF 5 MINUTES AND BE PRESENT, IN THE NOW. BREATHE.
- [ ] **EXERCISE** – DID YOU MOVE AT LEAST 30 MINUTES TODAY?
- [ ] **FUEL** – EAT 80% NUTRIENT DENSE FOOD THAT ENERGIZES YOU

I WAS MOST GRATEFUL FOR TODAY

Good Evening Gorgeous!

I LOVE TO GIVE. TODAY I GAVE

CHEERS TO ME!!!
LET'S CELEBRATE MY SUCCESSES FOR THE DAY

I AM BRILLIANT
gorgeous
TALENTED AND FABULOUS

GOOD MORNING gorgeous!

I AM GRATEFUL FOR

MY MANTRA *for today!*

FUN!!! TODAY FOR FUN I WILL

- ☐ VISUALIZATION - SET YOUR TIMER FOR A MINIMUM OF 5 MINUTES AND GO THERE!
- ☐ MEDITATION - SET YOUR TIMER FOR A MINIMUM OF 5 MINUTES AND BE PRESENT. IN THE NOW. BREATHE.
- ☐ EXERCISE - DID YOU MOVE AT LEAST 30 MINUTES TODAY?
- ☐ FUEL - EAT 80% NUTRIENT DENSE FOOD THAT ENERGIZES YOU

I WAS MOST GRATEFUL FOR TODAY

Good Evening Gorgeous!

I LOVE TO GIVE. TODAY I GAVE

CHEERS TO ME!!!
LET'S CELEBRATE MY SUCCESSES FOR THE DAY

I AM BRILLIANT
gorgeous
TALENTED AND FABULOUS

GOOD MORNING gorgeous!

I AM GRATEFUL FOR

MY MANTRA *for today!*

FUN!!! TODAY FOR FUN I WILL

- ☐ VISUALIZATION – SET YOUR TIMER FOR A MINIMUM OF 5 MINUTES AND GO THERE!
- ☐ MEDITATION – SET YOUR TIMER FOR A MINIMUM OF 5 MINUTES AND BE PRESENT, IN THE NOW. BREATHE.
- ☐ EXERCISE – DID YOU MOVE AT LEAST 30 MINUTES TODAY?
- ☐ FUEL – EAT 80% NUTRIENT DENSE FOOD THAT ENERGIZES YOU

I WAS MOST GRATEFUL FOR TODAY

Good Evening Gorgeous!

I LOVE TO GIVE. TODAY I GAVE

CHEERS TO ME!!!
LET'S CELEBRATE MY SUCCESSES FOR THE DAY

I AM BRILLIANT
gorgeous
TALENTED AND FABULOUS

GOOD MORNING gorgeous!

I AM GRATEFUL FOR

MY MANTRA for today!

FUN!!! TODAY FOR FUN I WILL

- ☐ **VISUALIZATION** – SET YOUR TIMER FOR A MINIMUM OF 5 MINUTES AND GO THERE!
- ☐ **MEDITATION** – SET YOUR TIMER FOR A MINIMUM OF 5 MINUTES AND BE PRESENT, IN THE NOW. BREATHE.
- ☐ **EXERCISE** – DID YOU MOVE AT LEAST 30 MINUTES TODAY?
- ☐ **FUEL** – EAT 80% NUTRIENT DENSE FOOD THAT ENERGIZES YOU

I WAS MOST GRATEFUL FOR TODAY

Good Evening Gorgeous!

I LOVE TO GIVE. TODAY I GAVE

CHEERS TO ME!!!
LET'S CELEBRATE MY SUCCESSES FOR THE DAY

I AM BRILLIANT
gorgeous
TALENTED AND FABULOUS

GOOD MORNING gorgeous!

I AM GRATEFUL FOR
....
....
....

MY MANTRA for today!
....
....
....
....

FUN!!! TODAY FOR FUN I WILL
....
....
....

- ☐ **VISUALIZATION** – SET YOUR TIMER FOR A MINIMUM OF 5 MINUTES AND GO THERE!
- ☐ **MEDITATION** – SET YOUR TIMER FOR A MINIMUM OF 5 MINUTES AND BE PRESENT, IN THE NOW. BREATHE.
- ☐ **EXERCISE** – DID YOU MOVE AT LEAST 30 MINUTES TODAY?
- ☐ **FUEL** – EAT 80% NUTRIENT DENSE FOOD THAT ENERGIZES YOU

I WAS MOST GRATEFUL FOR TODAY
....
....
....
....
....
....

Good Evening Gorgeous!

I LOVE TO GIVE. TODAY I GAVE
....
....
....

CHEERS TO ME!!!
LET'S CELEBRATE MY SUCCESSES FOR THE DAY
....
....
....

I AM BRILLIANT
gorgeous
TALENTED AND FABULOUS

GOOD MORNING gorgeous!

I AM GRATEFUL FOR

MY MANTRA *for today!*

FUN!!! TODAY FOR FUN I WILL

- ☐ VISUALIZATION - SET YOUR TIMER FOR A MINIMUM OF 5 MINUTES AND GO THERE!
- ☐ MEDITATION - SET YOUR TIMER FOR A MINIMUM OF 5 MINUTES AND BE PRESENT. IN THE NOW. BREATHE.
- ☐ EXERCISE - DID YOU MOVE AT LEAST 30 MINUTES TODAY?
- ☐ FUEL - EAT 80% NUTRIENT DENSE FOOD THAT ENERGIZES YOU

I WAS MOST GRATEFUL FOR TODAY

Good Evening Gorgeous!

I LOVE TO GIVE. TODAY I GAVE

CHEERS TO ME!!!
LET'S CELEBRATE MY SUCCESSES FOR THE DAY

I AM BRILLIANT
gorgeous
TALENTED AND FABULOUS

GOOD MORNING gorgeous!

I AM GRATEFUL FOR

MY MANTRA for today!

FUN!!! TODAY FOR FUN I WILL

- ☐ **VISUALIZATION** – SET YOUR TIMER FOR A MINIMUM OF 5 MINUTES AND GO THERE!
- ☐ **MEDITATION** – SET YOUR TIMER FOR A MINIMUM OF 5 MINUTES AND BE PRESENT, IN THE NOW. BREATHE.
- ☐ **EXERCISE** – DID YOU MOVE AT LEAST 30 MINUTES TODAY?
- ☐ **FUEL** – EAT 80% NUTRIENT DENSE FOOD THAT ENERGIZES YOU

I WAS MOST GRATEFUL FOR TODAY

Good Evening Gorgeous!

I LOVE TO GIVE. TODAY I GAVE

CHEERS TO ME!!!
LET'S CELEBRATE MY SUCCESSES FOR THE DAY

I AM BRILLIANT
gorgeous
TALENTED AND FABULOUS

GOOD MORNING gorgeous!

I AM GRATEFUL FOR
....
....
....

MY MANTRA *for today!*
....
....
....
....

FUN!!! TODAY FOR FUN I WILL
....
....
....

- ☐ **VISUALIZATION** – SET YOUR TIMER FOR A MINIMUM OF 5 MINUTES AND GO THERE!
- ☐ **MEDITATION** – SET YOUR TIMER FOR A MINIMUM OF 5 MINUTES AND BE PRESENT, IN THE NOW, BREATHE.
- ☐ **EXERCISE** – DID YOU MOVE AT LEAST 30 MINUTES TODAY?
- ☐ **FUEL** – EAT 80% NUTRIENT DENSE FOOD THAT ENERGIZES YOU

I WAS MOST GRATEFUL FOR TODAY
....
....
....
....
....

Good Evening Gorgeous!

I LOVE TO GIVE. TODAY I GAVE
....
....
....

CHEERS TO ME!!!
LET'S CELEBRATE MY SUCCESSES FOR THE DAY
....
....
....

I AM BRILLIANT
gorgeous
TALENTED AND FABULOUS

GOOD MORNING gorgeous!

I AM GRATEFUL FOR

MY MANTRA for today!

FUN!!! TODAY FOR FUN I WILL

- ☐ VISUALIZATION – SET YOUR TIMER FOR A MINIMUM OF 5 MINUTES AND GO THERE!
- ☐ MEDITATION – SET YOUR TIMER FOR A MINIMUM OF 5 MINUTES AND BE PRESENT, IN THE NOW. BREATHE.
- ☐ EXERCISE – DID YOU MOVE AT LEAST 30 MINUTES TODAY?
- ☐ FUEL – EAT 80% NUTRIENT DENSE FOOD THAT ENERGIZES YOU

I WAS MOST GRATEFUL FOR TODAY

Good Evening Gorgeous!

I LOVE TO GIVE. TODAY I GAVE

CHEERS TO ME!!!
LET'S CELEBRATE MY SUCCESSES FOR THE DAY

I AM BRILLIANT
gorgeous
TALENTED AND FABULOUS

GOOD MORNING gorgeous!

I AM GRATEFUL FOR

MY MANTRA for today!

FUN!!! TODAY FOR FUN I WILL

- [ ] **VISUALIZATION** – SET YOUR TIMER FOR A MINIMUM OF 5 MINUTES AND GO THERE!
- [ ] **MEDITATION** – SET YOUR TIMER FOR A MINIMUM OF 5 MINUTES AND BE PRESENT, IN THE NOW. BREATHE.
- [ ] **EXERCISE** – DID YOU MOVE AT LEAST 30 MINUTES TODAY?
- [ ] **FUEL** – EAT 80% NUTRIENT DENSE FOOD THAT ENERGIZES YOU

I WAS MOST GRATEFUL FOR TODAY

Good Evening Gorgeous!

I LOVE TO GIVE. TODAY I GAVE

CHEERS TO ME!!!
LET'S CELEBRATE MY SUCCESSES FOR THE DAY

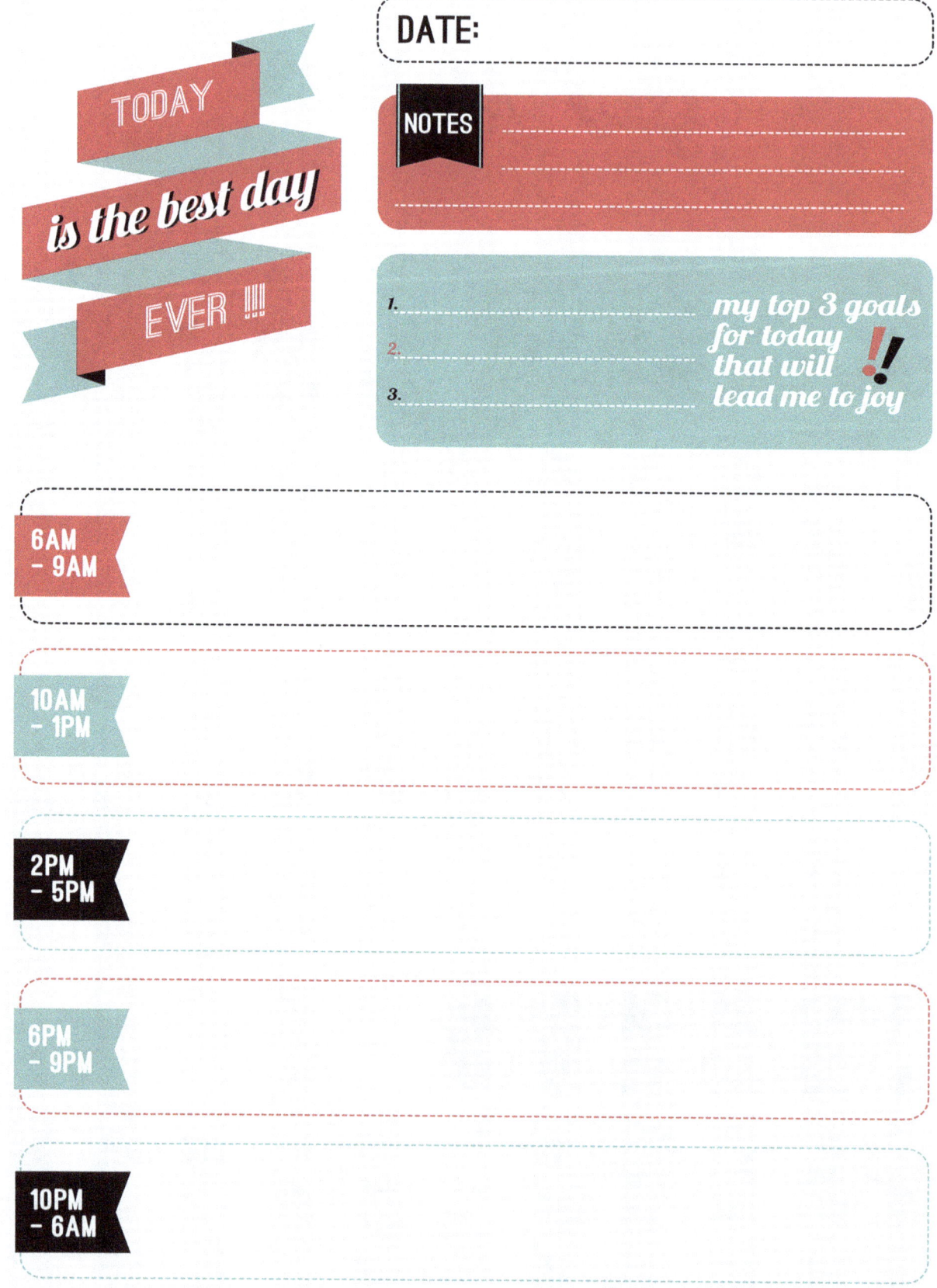

PAUSE CAFÉ
coffee break

time to pause and reflect. are you focused on your goals? need to revise your priorities? get more specific with your visualization? add some new mantras? grab a cup of hot coffee or tea and sit down and focus on your joyful plan for the next 30 days.

L'ART DE VIVRE!
VISUALIZE THE NEXT 30 DAYS

RAISON D'ÊTRE!
WHAT ARE YOUR TOP 2-3 PRIORITIES?

PAIN AU CHOCOLAT FOR YOUR BRAIN!
MANTRAS AND AFFIRMATIONS YOU NEED TO HEAR DAILY

LA VIE EST BELLE!
WHAT ARE YOU MOST GRATEFUL FOR FROM THE LAST 30 DAYS?

VIVRE LA VIE PAR LA CONCEPTION!
REVISIT YOUR 10 GOALS FOR THE YEAR
(THINGS CHANGE, PERSPECTIVE, PRIORITIES OR MAYBE YOU ACCOMPLISHED A GOAL AND WOULD LIKE TO ADD ANOTHER. OR, MAYBE THEY ARE THE SAME AND YOU NEED TO REWRITE THEM HERE)

I AM BRILLIANT

TALENTED AND FABULOUS

GOOD MORNING gorgeous!

I AM GRATEFUL FOR
....
....
....
....

 **MY MANTRA**
....
....
....
....

FUN!!! TODAY FOR FUN I WILL
....
....
....

☐ **VISUALIZATION** – SET YOUR TIMER FOR A MINIMUM OF 5 MINUTES AND GO THERE!

☐ **MEDITATION** – SET YOUR TIMER FOR A MINIMUM OF 5 MINUTES AND BE PRESENT, IN THE NOW. BREATHE.

☐ **EXERCISE** – DID YOU MOVE AT LEAST 30 MINUTES TODAY?

☐ **FUEL** – EAT 80% NUTRIENT DENSE FOOD THAT ENERGIZES YOU

I WAS MOST GRATEFUL FOR TODAY
....
....
....
....
....
....

Good Evening Gorgeous!

I LOVE TO GIVE. TODAY I GAVE
....
....
....
....

CHEERS TO ME!!!
LET'S CELEBRATE MY SUCCESSES FOR THE DAY
....
....
....
....

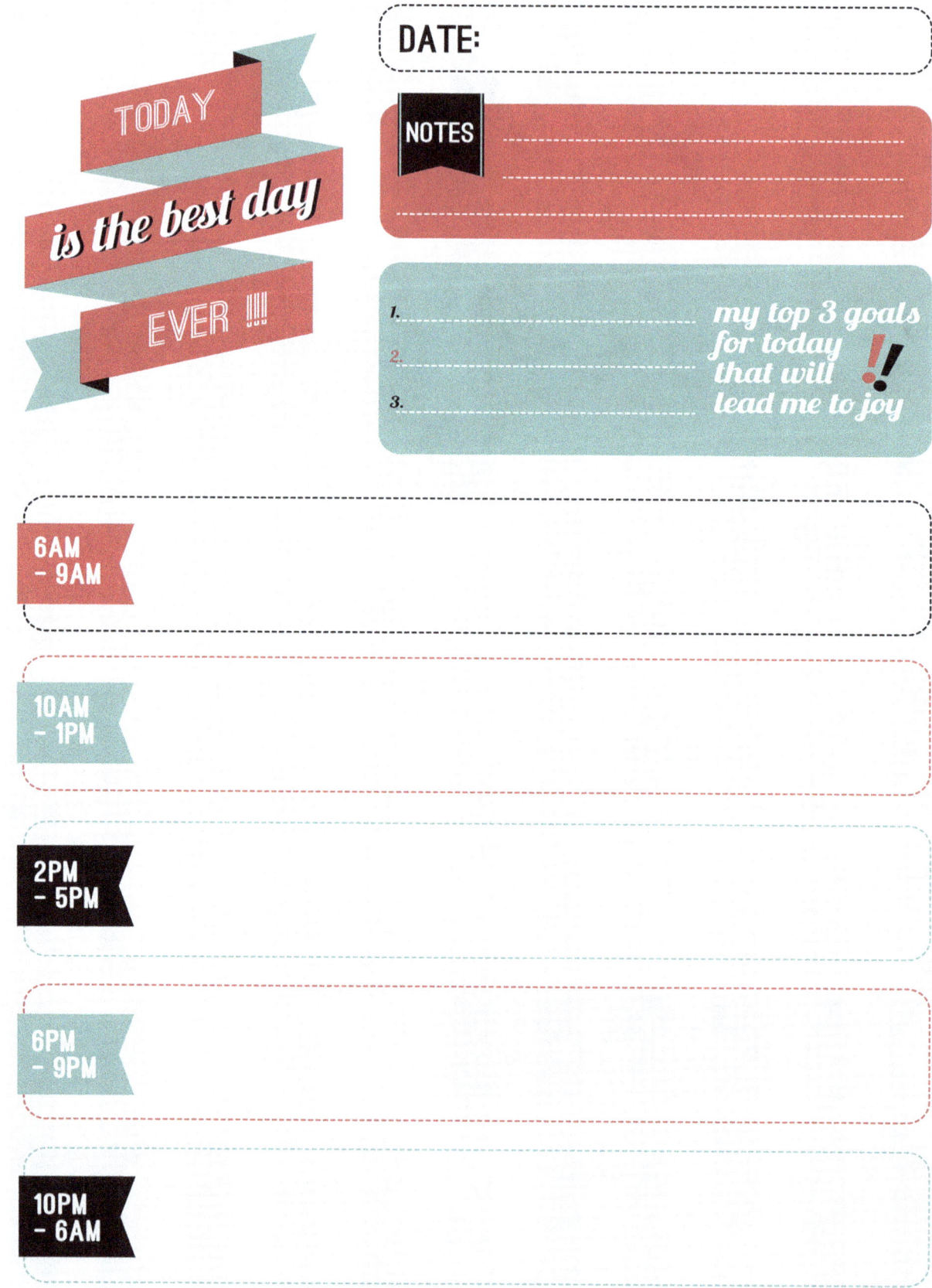

I AM BRILLIANT
gorgeous
TALENTED AND FABULOUS

GOOD MORNING gorgeous!

I AM GRATEFUL FOR

MY MANTRA
for today!

FUN!!! TODAY FOR FUN I WILL

- ☐ VISUALIZATION – SET YOUR TIMER FOR A MINIMUM OF 5 MINUTES AND GO THERE!
- ☐ MEDITATION – SET YOUR TIMER FOR A MINIMUM OF 5 MINUTES AND BE PRESENT, IN THE NOW. BREATHE.
- ☐ EXERCISE – DID YOU MOVE AT LEAST 30 MINUTES TODAY?
- ☐ FUEL – EAT 80% NUTRIENT DENSE FOOD THAT ENERGIZES YOU

I WAS MOST GRATEFUL FOR TODAY

Good Evening Gorgeous!

I LOVE TO GIVE. TODAY I GAVE

CHEERS TO ME!!!
LET'S CELEBRATE MY SUCCESSES FOR THE DAY

I AM BRILLIANT
gorgeous
TALENTED AND FABULOUS

GOOD MORNING gorgeous!

I AM GRATEFUL FOR

_____
_____
_____

MY MANTRA *for today!*

_____
_____
_____
_____

FUN!!! TODAY FOR FUN I WILL

_____
_____

- ☐ **VISUALIZATION** – SET YOUR TIMER FOR A MINIMUM OF 5 MINUTES AND GO THERE!
- ☐ **MEDITATION** – SET YOUR TIMER FOR A MINIMUM OF 5 MINUTES AND BE PRESENT, IN THE NOW. BREATHE.
- ☐ **EXERCISE** – DID YOU MOVE AT LEAST 30 MINUTES TODAY?
- ☐ **FUEL** – EAT 80% NUTRIENT DENSE FOOD THAT ENERGIZES YOU

I WAS MOST GRATEFUL FOR TODAY

_____
_____
_____
_____
_____

Good Evening Gorgeous!

I LOVE TO GIVE. TODAY I GAVE

_____
_____
_____

CHEERS TO ME!!!
LET'S CELEBRATE MY SUCCESSES FOR THE DAY

_____
_____
_____

I AM BRILLIANT
gorgeous
TALENTED AND FABULOUS

GOOD MORNING gorgeous!

I AM GRATEFUL FOR

MY MANTRA for today!

FUN!!! TODAY FOR FUN I WILL

- ☐ VISUALIZATION – SET YOUR TIMER FOR A MINIMUM OF 5 MINUTES AND GO THERE!
- ☐ MEDITATION – SET YOUR TIMER FOR A MINIMUM OF 5 MINUTES AND BE PRESENT, IN THE NOW. BREATHE.
- ☐ EXERCISE – DID YOU MOVE AT LEAST 30 MINUTES TODAY?
- ☐ FUEL – EAT 80% NUTRIENT DENSE FOOD THAT ENERGIZES YOU

I WAS MOST GRATEFUL FOR TODAY

Good Evening Gorgeous!

I LOVE TO GIVE. TODAY I GAVE

CHEERS TO ME!!!
LET'S CELEBRATE MY SUCCESSES FOR THE DAY

DATE:

NOTES

1. _____
2. _____
3. _____

my top 3 goals for today that will lead me to joy!!

6AM – 9AM

10AM – 1PM

2PM – 5PM

6PM – 9PM

10PM – 6AM

*make sure you get your sleep!

I AM BRILLIANT
gorgeous
TALENTED AND FABULOUS

GOOD MORNING gorgeous!

I AM GRATEFUL FOR

MY MANTRA *for today!*

FUN!!! TODAY FOR FUN I WILL

- ☐ VISUALIZATION – SET YOUR TIMER FOR A MINIMUM OF 5 MINUTES AND GO THERE!
- ☐ MEDITATION – SET YOUR TIMER FOR A MINIMUM OF 5 MINUTES AND BE PRESENT, IN THE NOW. BREATHE.
- ☐ EXERCISE – DID YOU MOVE AT LEAST 30 MINUTES TODAY?
- ☐ FUEL – EAT 80% NUTRIENT DENSE FOOD THAT ENERGIZES YOU

I WAS MOST GRATEFUL FOR TODAY

Good Evening Gorgeous!

I LOVE TO GIVE. TODAY I GAVE

CHEERS TO ME!!!
LET'S CELEBRATE MY SUCCESSES FOR THE DAY

I AM BRILLIANT
gorgeous
TALENTED AND FABULOUS

GOOD MORNING gorgeous!

I AM GRATEFUL FOR

MY MANTRA for today!

FUN!!! TODAY FOR FUN I WILL

- [ ] VISUALIZATION – SET YOUR TIMER FOR A MINIMUM OF 5 MINUTES AND GO THERE!
- [ ] MEDITATION – SET YOUR TIMER FOR A MINIMUM OF 5 MINUTES AND BE PRESENT, IN THE NOW. BREATHE.
- [ ] EXERCISE – DID YOU MOVE AT LEAST 30 MINUTES TODAY?
- [ ] FUEL – EAT 80% NUTRIENT DENSE FOOD THAT ENERGIZES YOU

I WAS MOST GRATEFUL FOR TODAY

Good Evening Gorgeous!

I LOVE TO GIVE. TODAY I GAVE

CHEERS TO ME!!!
LET'S CELEBRATE MY SUCCESSES FOR THE DAY

I AM BRILLIANT
gorgeous
TALENTED AND FABULOUS

GOOD MORNING gorgeous!

I AM GRATEFUL FOR

 **MY MANTRA**

 **for today!**

FUN!!! TODAY FOR FUN I WILL

- [ ] VISUALIZATION – SET YOUR TIMER FOR A MINIMUM OF 5 MINUTES AND GO THERE!
- [ ] MEDITATION – SET YOUR TIMER FOR A MINIMUM OF 5 MINUTES AND BE PRESENT, IN THE NOW. BREATHE.
- [ ] EXERCISE – DID YOU MOVE AT LEAST 30 MINUTES TODAY?
- [ ] FUEL – EAT 80% NUTRIENT DENSE FOOD THAT ENERGIZES YOU

I WAS MOST GRATEFUL FOR TODAY

Good Evening Gorgeous!

I LOVE TO GIVE. TODAY I GAVE

CHEERS TO ME!!!
LET'S CELEBRATE MY SUCCESSES FOR THE DAY

I AM GRATEFUL FOR

FUN!!! TODAY FOR FUN I WILL

- [ ] VISUALIZATION – SET YOUR TIMER FOR A MINIMUM OF 5 MINUTES AND GO THERE!
- [ ] MEDITATION – SET YOUR TIMER FOR A MINIMUM OF 5 MINUTES AND BE PRESENT, IN THE NOW. BREATHE.
- [ ] EXERCISE – DID YOU MOVE AT LEAST 30 MINUTES TODAY?
- [ ] FUEL – EAT 80% NUTRIENT DENSE FOOD THAT ENERGIZES YOU

I WAS MOST GRATEFUL FOR TODAY

Good Evening Gorgeous!

I LOVE TO GIVE. TODAY I GAVE

CHEERS TO ME!!!
LET'S CELEBRATE MY SUCCESSES FOR THE DAY

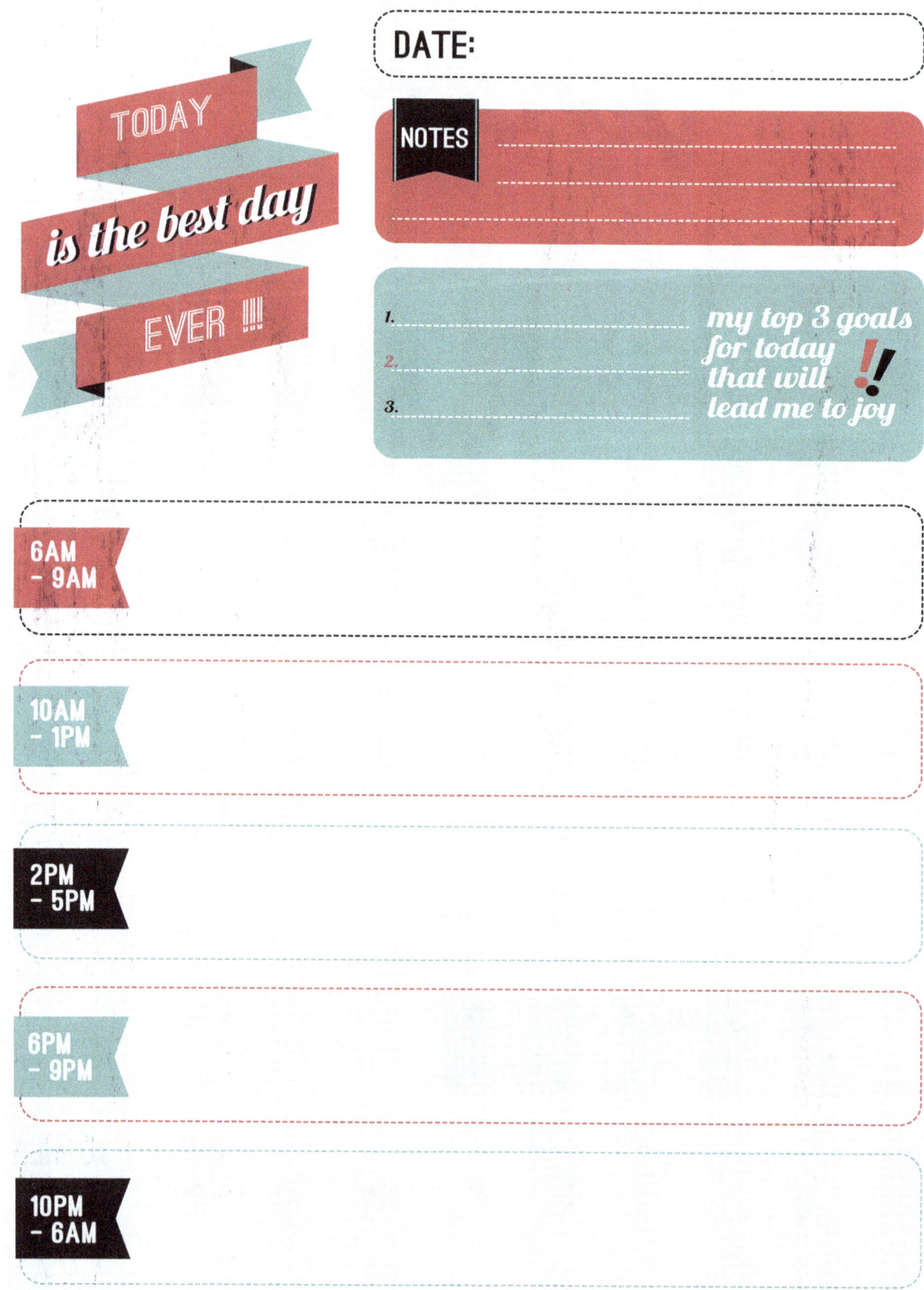

I AM BRILLIANT
gorgeous
TALENTED AND FABULOUS

GOOD MORNING gorgeous!

I AM GRATEFUL FOR

MY MANTRA for today!

FUN!!! TODAY FOR FUN I WILL

- [ ] VISUALIZATION - SET YOUR TIMER FOR A MINIMUM OF 5 MINUTES AND GO THERE!
- [ ] MEDITATION - SET YOUR TIMER FOR A MINIMUM OF 5 MINUTES AND BE PRESENT, IN THE NOW. BREATHE.
- [ ] EXERCISE - DID YOU MOVE AT LEAST 30 MINUTES TODAY?
- [ ] FUEL - EAT 80% NUTRIENT DENSE FOOD THAT ENERGIZES YOU

I WAS MOST GRATEFUL FOR TODAY

Good Evening Gorgeous!

I LOVE TO GIVE. TODAY I GAVE

CHEERS TO ME!!!
LET'S CELEBRATE MY SUCCESSES FOR THE DAY

I AM BRILLIANT
gorgeous
TALENTED AND FABULOUS

GOOD MORNING gorgeous!

I AM GRATEFUL FOR

MY MANTRA *for today!*

FUN!!! TODAY FOR FUN I WILL

☐ **VISUALIZATION** – SET YOUR TIMER FOR A MINIMUM OF 5 MINUTES AND GO THERE!

☐ **MEDITATION** – SET YOUR TIMER FOR A MINIMUM OF 5 MINUTES AND BE PRESENT, IN THE NOW. BREATHE.

☐ **EXERCISE** – DID YOU MOVE AT LEAST 30 MINUTES TODAY?

☐ **FUEL** – EAT 80% NUTRIENT DENSE FOOD THAT ENERGIZES YOU

I WAS MOST GRATEFUL FOR TODAY

Good Evening Gorgeous!

I LOVE TO GIVE. TODAY I GAVE

CHEERS TO ME!!!
LET'S CELEBRATE MY SUCCESSES FOR THE DAY

I AM BRILLIANT
gorgeous
TALENTED AND FABULOUS

GOOD MORNING gorgeous!

I AM GRATEFUL FOR
....
....
....
....

MY MANTRA for today!
....
....
....
....

FUN!!! TODAY FOR FUN I WILL
....
....
....

- ☐ **VISUALIZATION** – SET YOUR TIMER FOR A MINIMUM OF 5 MINUTES AND GO THERE!
- ☐ **MEDITATION** – SET YOUR TIMER FOR A MINIMUM OF 5 MINUTES AND BE PRESENT, IN THE NOW. BREATHE.
- ☐ **EXERCISE** – DID YOU MOVE AT LEAST 30 MINUTES TODAY?
- ☐ **FUEL** – EAT 80% NUTRIENT DENSE FOOD THAT ENERGIZES YOU

I WAS MOST GRATEFUL FOR TODAY
....
....
....
....
....

Good Evening Gorgeous!

I LOVE TO GIVE. TODAY I GAVE
....
....
....

CHEERS TO ME!!!
LET'S CELEBRATE MY SUCCESSES FOR THE DAY
....
....
....

I AM BRILLIANT
gorgeous
TALENTED AND FABULOUS

GOOD MORNING gorgeous!

I AM GRATEFUL FOR

_____
_____
_____

MY MANTRA for today!

_____
_____
_____

FUN!!! TODAY FOR FUN I WILL
_____
_____
_____

- ☐ **VISUALIZATION** – SET YOUR TIMER FOR A MINIMUM OF 5 MINUTES AND GO THERE!
- ☐ **MEDITATION** – SET YOUR TIMER FOR A MINIMUM OF 5 MINUTES AND BE PRESENT, IN THE NOW. BREATHE.
- ☐ **EXERCISE** – DID YOU MOVE AT LEAST 30 MINUTES TODAY?
- ☐ **FUEL** – EAT 80% NUTRIENT DENSE FOOD THAT ENERGIZES YOU

I WAS MOST GRATEFUL FOR TODAY
_____
_____
_____
_____
_____

Good Evening Gorgeous!

I LOVE TO GIVE. TODAY I GAVE
_____
_____
_____

CHEERS TO ME!!!
LET'S CELEBRATE MY SUCCESSES FOR THE DAY
_____
_____
_____

I AM BRILLIANT
gorgeous
TALENTED AND FABULOUS

GOOD MORNING gorgeous!

I AM GRATEFUL FOR
_____
_____
_____

MY MANTRA for today!
_____
_____
_____
_____

FUN!!! TODAY FOR FUN I WILL
_____
_____
_____

- ☐ **VISUALIZATION** – SET YOUR TIMER FOR A MINIMUM OF 5 MINUTES AND GO THERE!
- ☐ **MEDITATION** – SET YOUR TIMER FOR A MINIMUM OF 5 MINUTES AND BE PRESENT. IN THE NOW. BREATHE.
- ☐ **EXERCISE** – DID YOU MOVE AT LEAST 30 MINUTES TODAY?
- ☐ **FUEL** – EAT 80% NUTRIENT DENSE FOOD THAT ENERGIZES YOU

I WAS MOST GRATEFUL FOR TODAY
_____
_____
_____
_____
_____
_____

Good Evening Gorgeous!

I LOVE TO GIVE. TODAY I GAVE
_____
_____
_____

CHEERS TO ME!!!
LET'S CELEBRATE MY SUCCESSES FOR THE DAY
_____
_____
_____

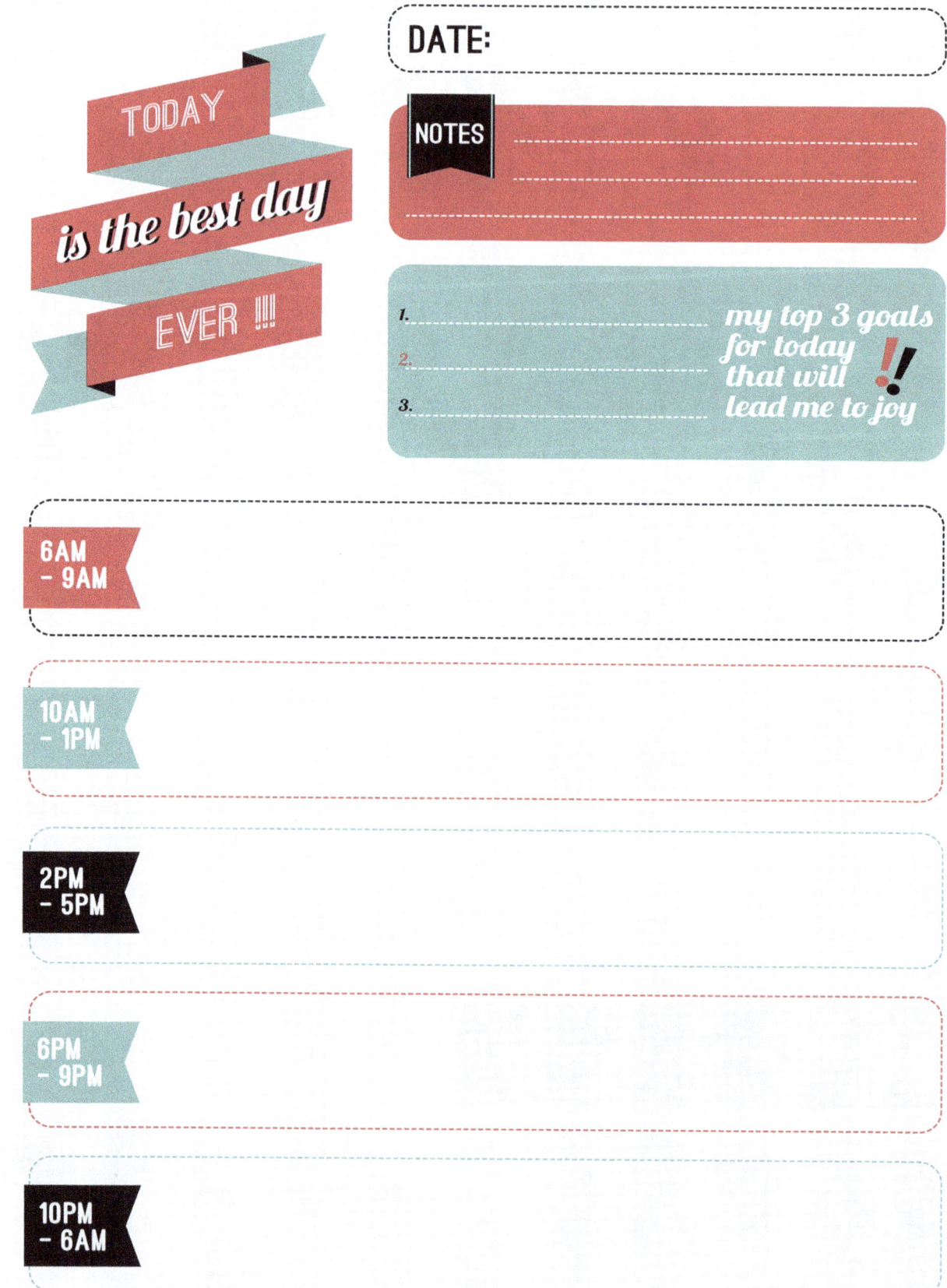

I AM BRILLIANT
gorgeous
TALENTED AND FABULOUS

GOOD MORNING gorgeous!

MY MANTRA for today!

....
....
....

I AM GRATEFUL FOR
....
....
....

FUN!!! TODAY FOR FUN I WILL
....
....
....

- ☐ **VISUALIZATION** – SET YOUR TIMER FOR A MINIMUM OF 5 MINUTES AND GO THERE!
- ☐ **MEDITATION** – SET YOUR TIMER FOR A MINIMUM OF 5 MINUTES AND BE PRESENT, IN THE NOW. BREATHE.
- ☐ **EXERCISE** – DID YOU MOVE AT LEAST 30 MINUTES TODAY?
- ☐ **FUEL** – EAT 80% NUTRIENT DENSE FOOD THAT ENERGIZES YOU

I WAS MOST GRATEFUL FOR TODAY
....
....
....
....
....

Good Evening Gorgeous!

I LOVE TO GIVE. TODAY I GAVE
....
....

CHEERS TO ME!!!
LET'S CELEBRATE MY SUCCESSES FOR THE DAY
....
....

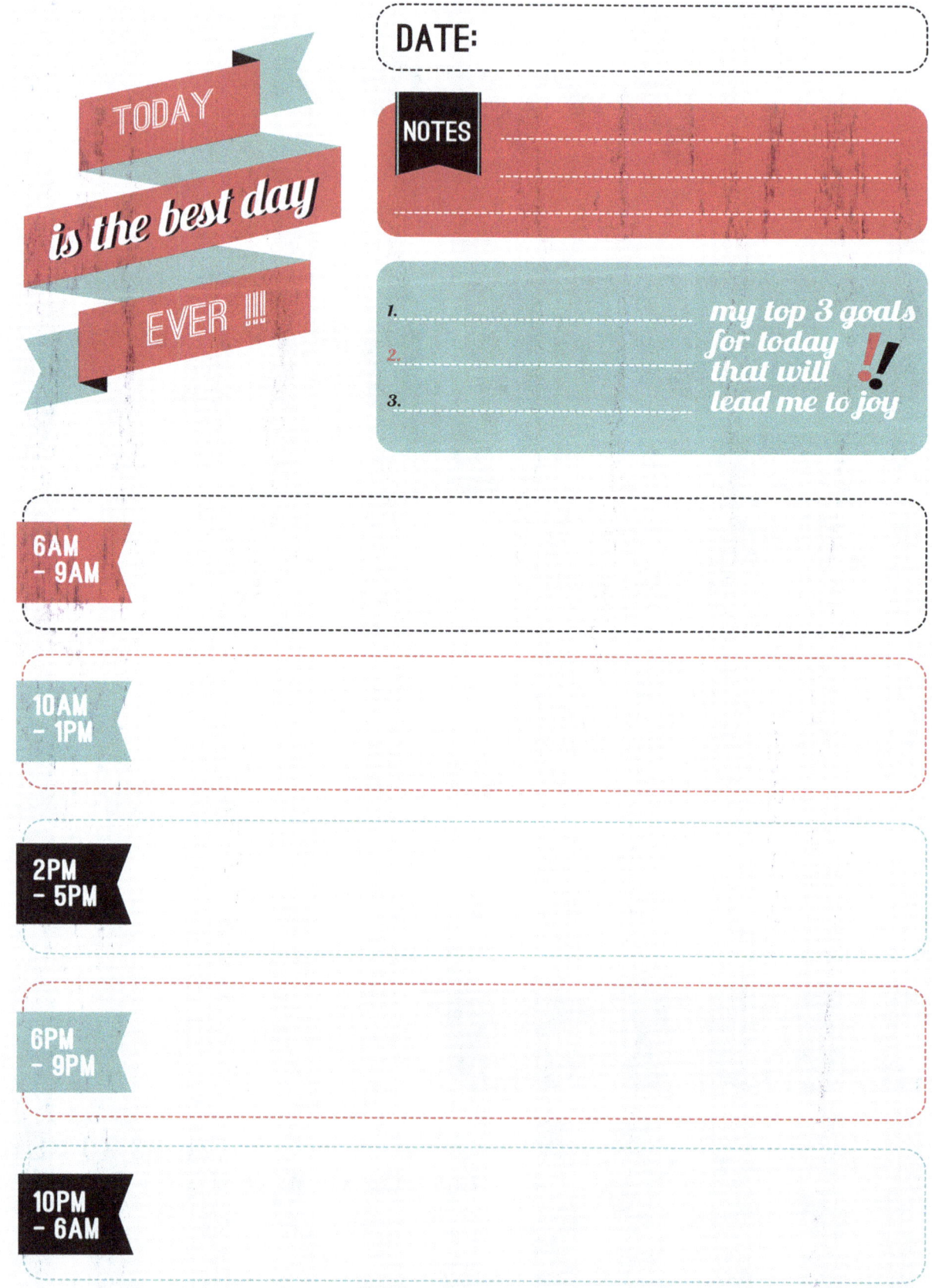

I AM BRILLIANT
gorgeous
TALENTED AND FABULOUS

GOOD MORNING *gorgeous!*

I AM GRATEFUL FOR

 **MY MANTRA**  *for today!*

FUN!!! TODAY FOR FUN I WILL

- ☐ VISUALIZATION – SET YOUR TIMER FOR A MINIMUM OF 5 MINUTES AND GO THERE!
- ☐ MEDITATION – SET YOUR TIMER FOR A MINIMUM OF 5 MINUTES AND BE PRESENT, IN THE NOW. BREATHE.
- ☐ EXERCISE – DID YOU MOVE AT LEAST 30 MINUTES TODAY?
- ☐ FUEL – EAT 80% NUTRIENT DENSE FOOD THAT ENERGIZES YOU

I WAS MOST GRATEFUL FOR TODAY

Good Evening Gorgeous!

I LOVE TO GIVE. TODAY I GAVE

CHEERS TO ME!!!
LET'S CELEBRATE MY SUCCESSES FOR THE DAY

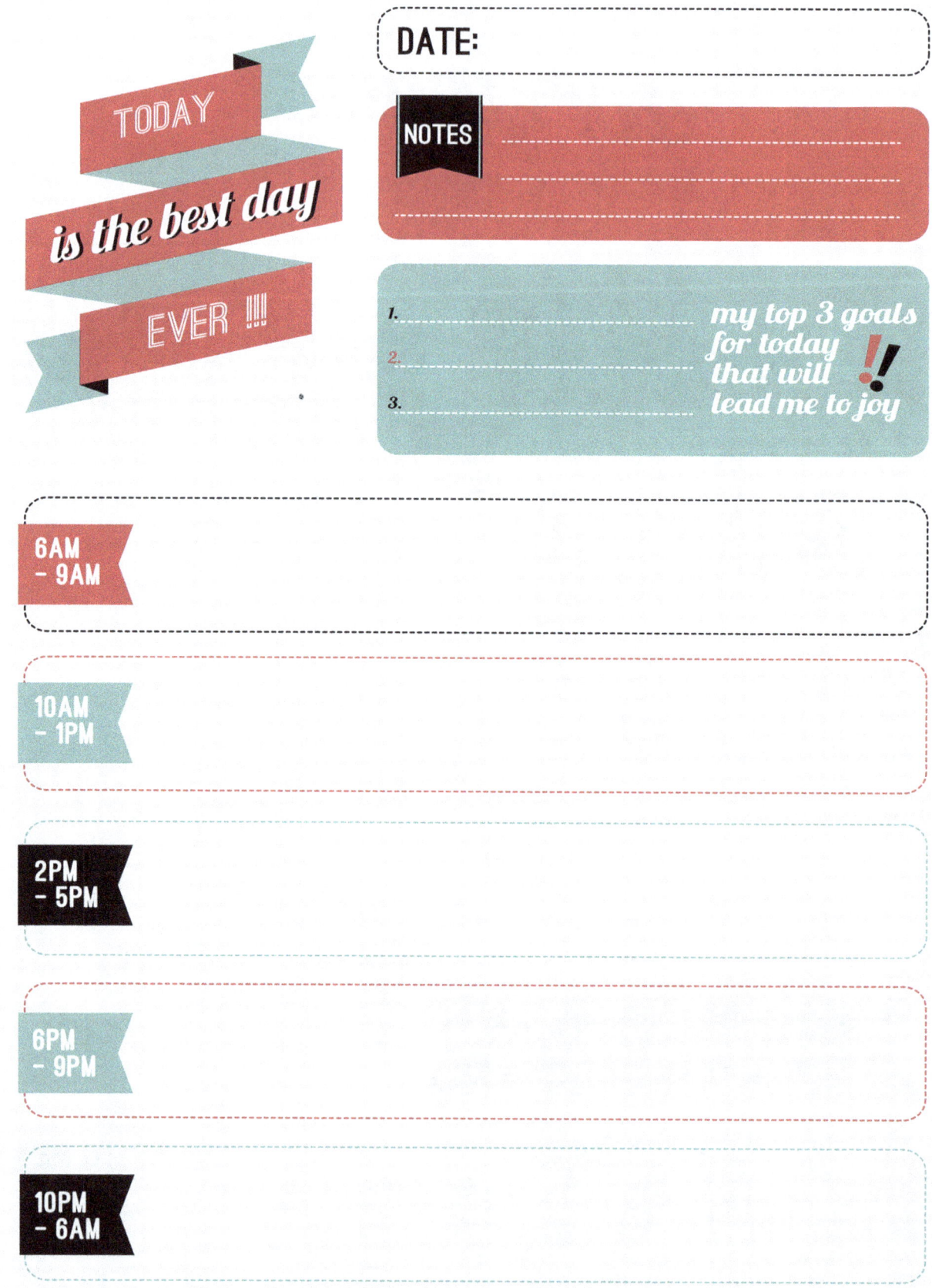

I AM BRILLIANT
gorgeous
TALENTED AND FABULOUS

GOOD MORNING gorgeous!

I AM GRATEFUL FOR
_____
_____
_____

MY MANTRA *for today!*
_____
_____
_____
_____

FUN!!! TODAY FOR FUN I WILL
_____
_____
_____

☐ **VISUALIZATION** – SET YOUR TIMER FOR A MINIMUM OF 5 MINUTES AND GO THERE!
☐ **MEDITATION** – SET YOUR TIMER FOR A MINIMUM OF 5 MINUTES AND BE PRESENT, IN THE NOW. BREATHE.
☐ **EXERCISE** – DID YOU MOVE AT LEAST 30 MINUTES TODAY?
☐ **FUEL** – EAT 80% NUTRIENT DENSE FOOD THAT ENERGIZES YOU

I WAS MOST GRATEFUL FOR TODAY
_____
_____
_____
_____
_____
_____

Good Evening Gorgeous!

I LOVE TO GIVE. TODAY I GAVE
_____
_____
_____

CHEERS TO ME!!!
LET'S CELEBRATE MY SUCCESSES FOR THE DAY
_____
_____
_____

I AM BRILLIANT
gorgeous
TALENTED AND FABULOUS

FUN!!! TODAY FOR FUN I WILL

☐ **VISUALIZATION** – SET YOUR TIMER FOR A MINIMUM OF 5 MINUTES AND GO THERE!

☐ **MEDITATION** – SET YOUR TIMER FOR A MINIMUM OF 5 MINUTES AND BE PRESENT, IN THE NOW. BREATHE.

☐ **EXERCISE** – DID YOU MOVE AT LEAST 30 MINUTES TODAY?

☐ **FUEL** – EAT 80% NUTRIENT DENSE FOOD THAT ENERGIZES YOU

I WAS MOST GRATEFUL FOR TODAY

Good Evening Gorgeous!

CHEERS TO ME!!!
LET'S CELEBRATE MY SUCCESSES FOR THE DAY

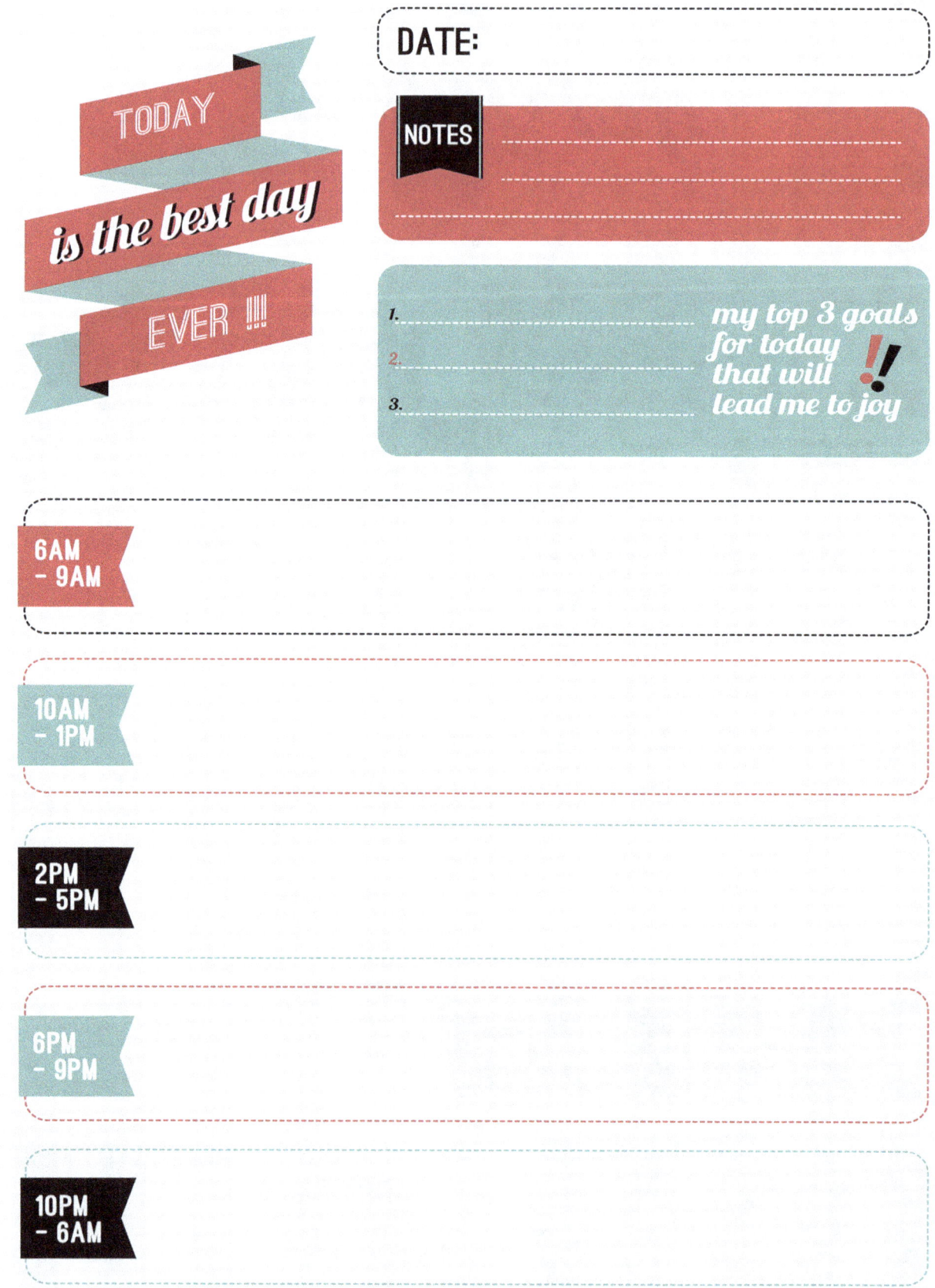

I AM BRILLIANT
gorgeous
TALENTED AND FABULOUS

GOOD MORNING gorgeous!

I AM GRATEFUL FOR

MY MANTRA for today!

FUN!!! TODAY FOR FUN I WILL

- [ ] **VISUALIZATION** – SET YOUR TIMER FOR A MINIMUM OF 5 MINUTES AND GO THERE!
- [ ] **MEDITATION** – SET YOUR TIMER FOR A MINIMUM OF 5 MINUTES AND BE PRESENT, IN THE NOW. BREATHE.
- [ ] **EXERCISE** – DID YOU MOVE AT LEAST 30 MINUTES TODAY?
- [ ] **FUEL** – EAT 80% NUTRIENT DENSE FOOD THAT ENERGIZES YOU

I WAS MOST GRATEFUL FOR TODAY

Good Evening Gorgeous!

I LOVE TO GIVE. TODAY I GAVE

CHEERS TO ME!!!
LET'S CELEBRATE MY SUCCESSES FOR THE DAY

GOOD MORNING gorgeous!

I AM GRATEFUL FOR

MY MANTRA — *for today!*

FUN!!! TODAY FOR FUN I WILL

- ☐ VISUALIZATION – SET YOUR TIMER FOR A MINIMUM OF 5 MINUTES AND GO THERE!
- ☐ MEDITATION – SET YOUR TIMER FOR A MINIMUM OF 5 MINUTES AND BE PRESENT, IN THE NOW. BREATHE.
- ☐ EXERCISE – DID YOU MOVE AT LEAST 30 MINUTES TODAY?
- ☐ FUEL – EAT 80% NUTRIENT DENSE FOOD THAT ENERGIZES YOU

I WAS MOST GRATEFUL FOR TODAY

Good Evening Gorgeous!

I LOVE TO GIVE. TODAY I GAVE

CHEERS TO ME!!!
LET'S CELEBRATE MY SUCCESSES FOR THE DAY

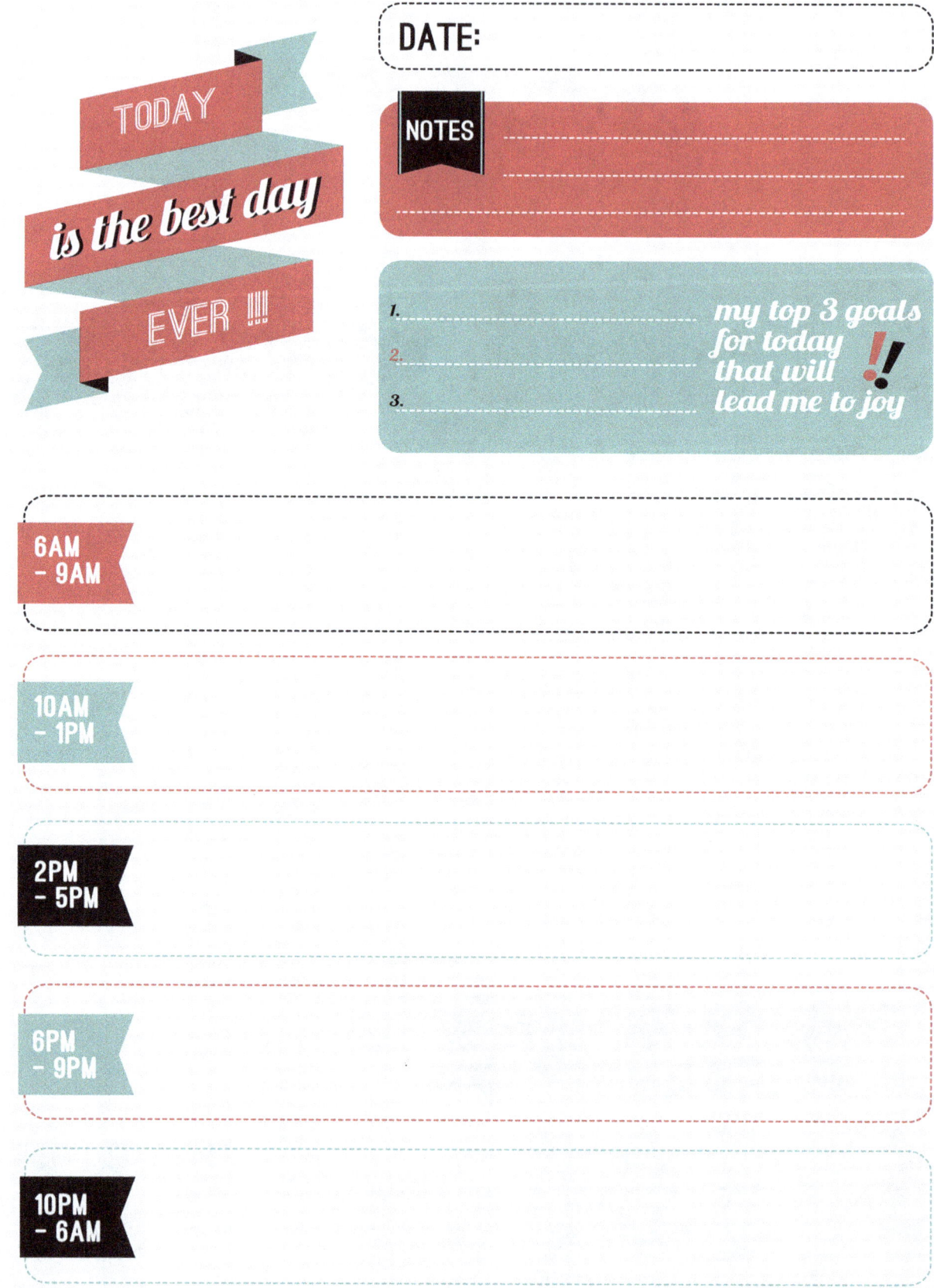

I AM BRILLIANT
gorgeous
TALENTED AND FABULOUS

GOOD MORNING gorgeous!

I AM GRATEFUL FOR

MY MANTRA *for today!*

FUN!!! TODAY FOR FUN I WILL

- [ ] **VISUALIZATION** – SET YOUR TIMER FOR A MINIMUM OF 5 MINUTES AND GO THERE!
- [ ] **MEDITATION** – SET YOUR TIMER FOR A MINIMUM OF 5 MINUTES AND BE PRESENT, IN THE NOW. BREATHE.
- [ ] **EXERCISE** – DID YOU MOVE AT LEAST 30 MINUTES TODAY?
- [ ] **FUEL** – EAT 80% NUTRIENT DENSE FOOD THAT ENERGIZES YOU

I WAS MOST GRATEFUL FOR TODAY

Good Evening Gorgeous!

I LOVE TO GIVE. TODAY I GAVE

CHEERS TO ME!!!
LET'S CELEBRATE MY SUCCESSES FOR THE DAY

I AM BRILLIANT
gorgeous
TALENTED AND FABULOUS

GOOD MORNING gorgeous!

I AM GRATEFUL FOR
....
....
....

MY MANTRA for today!
....
....
....
....

FUN!!! TODAY FOR FUN I WILL
....
....

- ☐ **VISUALIZATION** – SET YOUR TIMER FOR A MINIMUM OF 5 MINUTES AND GO THERE!
- ☐ **MEDITATION** – SET YOUR TIMER FOR A MINIMUM OF 5 MINUTES AND BE PRESENT, IN THE NOW. BREATHE.
- ☐ **EXERCISE** – DID YOU MOVE AT LEAST 30 MINUTES TODAY?
- ☐ **FUEL** – EAT 80% NUTRIENT DENSE FOOD THAT ENERGIZES YOU

I WAS MOST GRATEFUL FOR TODAY
....
....
....
....
....
....

Good Evening Gorgeous!

I LOVE TO GIVE. TODAY I GAVE
....
....
....

CHEERS TO ME!!!
LET'S CELEBRATE MY SUCCESSES FOR THE DAY
....
....
....

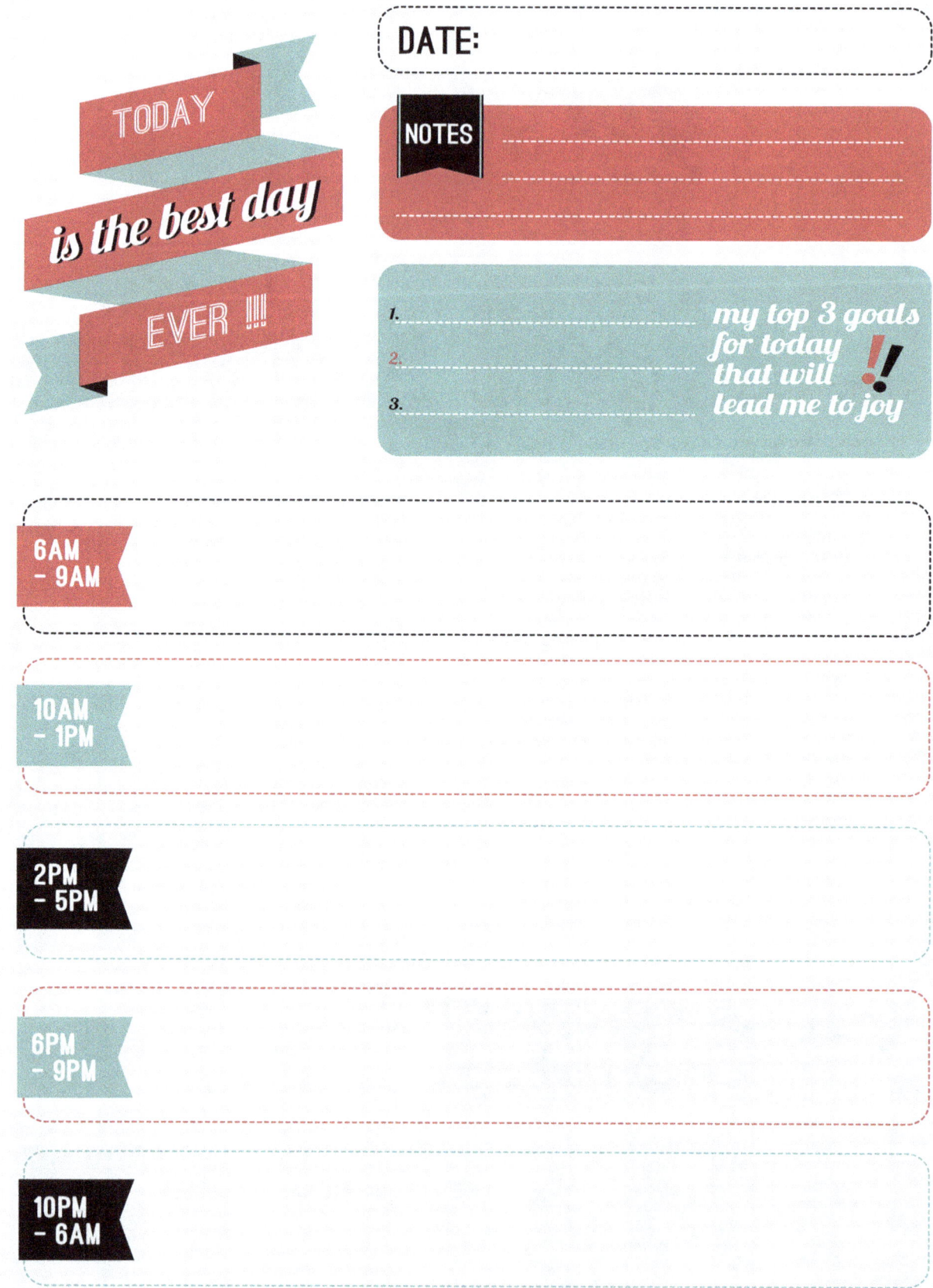

I AM BRILLIANT
gorgeous
TALENTED AND FABULOUS

GOOD MORNING gorgeous!

I AM GRATEFUL FOR

_____
_____
_____

MY MANTRA for today!

_____
_____
_____
_____

FUN!!! TODAY FOR FUN I WILL
_____
_____
_____

- [ ] **VISUALIZATION** – SET YOUR TIMER FOR A MINIMUM OF 5 MINUTES AND GO THERE!
- [ ] **MEDITATION** – SET YOUR TIMER FOR A MINIMUM OF 5 MINUTES AND BE PRESENT. IN THE NOW. BREATHE.
- [ ] **EXERCISE** – DID YOU MOVE AT LEAST 30 MINUTES TODAY?
- [ ] **FUEL** – EAT 80% NUTRIENT DENSE FOOD THAT ENERGIZES YOU

I WAS MOST GRATEFUL FOR TODAY
_____
_____
_____
_____
_____
_____

Good Evening Gorgeous!

I LOVE TO GIVE. TODAY I GAVE
_____
_____
_____

CHEERS TO ME!!!
LET'S CELEBRATE MY SUCCESSES FOR THE DAY
_____
_____
_____

I AM BRILLIANT
gorgeous
TALENTED AND FABULOUS

I AM GRATEFUL FOR

FUN!!! TODAY FOR FUN I WILL

- ☐ VISUALIZATION – SET YOUR TIMER FOR A MINIMUM OF 5 MINUTES AND GO THERE!
- ☐ MEDITATION – SET YOUR TIMER FOR A MINIMUM OF 5 MINUTES AND BE PRESENT, IN THE NOW. BREATHE.
- ☐ EXERCISE – DID YOU MOVE AT LEAST 30 MINUTES TODAY?
- ☐ FUEL – EAT 80% NUTRIENT DENSE FOOD THAT ENERGIZES YOU

I WAS MOST GRATEFUL FOR TODAY

I LOVE TO GIVE. TODAY I GAVE

CHEERS TO ME!!!
LET'S CELEBRATE MY SUCCESSES FOR THE DAY

TODAY *is the best day* **EVER !!!**

DATE:

NOTES

1.
2.
3.

my top 3 goals for today that will lead me to joy !!

6AM – 9AM

10AM – 1PM

2PM – 5PM

6PM – 9PM

10PM – 6AM

make sure you get your sleep!

I AM BRILLIANT
gorgeous
TALENTED AND FABULOUS

GOOD MORNING gorgeous!

I AM GRATEFUL FOR

MY MANTRA *for today!*

FUN!!! TODAY FOR FUN I WILL

- ☐ VISUALIZATION – SET YOUR TIMER FOR A MINIMUM OF 5 MINUTES AND GO THERE!
- ☐ MEDITATION – SET YOUR TIMER FOR A MINIMUM OF 5 MINUTES AND BE PRESENT, IN THE NOW. BREATHE.
- ☐ EXERCISE – DID YOU MOVE AT LEAST 30 MINUTES TODAY?
- ☐ FUEL – EAT 80% NUTRIENT DENSE FOOD THAT ENERGIZES YOU

I WAS MOST GRATEFUL FOR TODAY

Good Evening Gorgeous!

I LOVE TO GIVE. TODAY I GAVE

CHEERS TO ME!!!
LET'S CELEBRATE MY SUCCESSES FOR THE DAY

I AM BRILLIANT
gorgeous
TALENTED AND FABULOUS

GOOD MORNING gorgeous!

I AM GRATEFUL FOR

MY MANTRA for today!

FUN!!! TODAY FOR FUN I WILL

- [ ] **VISUALIZATION** - SET YOUR TIMER FOR A MINIMUM OF 5 MINUTES AND GO THERE!
- [ ] **MEDITATION** - SET YOUR TIMER FOR A MINIMUM OF 5 MINUTES AND BE PRESENT, IN THE NOW. BREATHE.
- [ ] **EXERCISE** - DID YOU MOVE AT LEAST 30 MINUTES TODAY?
- [ ] **FUEL** - EAT 80% NUTRIENT DENSE FOOD THAT ENERGIZES YOU

I WAS MOST GRATEFUL FOR TODAY

Good Evening Gorgeous!

I LOVE TO GIVE. TODAY I GAVE

CHEERS TO ME!!!
LET'S CELEBRATE MY SUCCESSES FOR THE DAY

I AM BRILLIANT
gorgeous
TALENTED AND FABULOUS

GOOD MORNING gorgeous!

I AM GRATEFUL FOR

MY MANTRA for today!

FUN!!! TODAY FOR FUN I WILL

- ☐ VISUALIZATION – SET YOUR TIMER FOR A MINIMUM OF 5 MINUTES AND GO THERE!
- ☐ MEDITATION – SET YOUR TIMER FOR A MINIMUM OF 5 MINUTES AND BE PRESENT, IN THE NOW. BREATHE.
- ☐ EXERCISE – DID YOU MOVE AT LEAST 30 MINUTES TODAY?
- ☐ FUEL – EAT 80% NUTRIENT DENSE FOOD THAT ENERGIZES YOU

I WAS MOST GRATEFUL FOR TODAY

Good Evening Gorgeous!

I LOVE TO GIVE. TODAY I GAVE

CHEERS TO ME!!!
LET'S CELEBRATE MY SUCCESSES FOR THE DAY

I AM BRILLIANT
gorgeous
TALENTED AND FABULOUS

GOOD MORNING *gorgeous!*

I AM GRATEFUL FOR

MY MANTRA *for today!*

FUN!!! TODAY FOR FUN I WILL

- [ ] **VISUALIZATION** – SET YOUR TIMER FOR A MINIMUM OF 5 MINUTES AND GO THERE!
- [ ] **MEDITATION** – SET YOUR TIMER FOR A MINIMUM OF 5 MINUTES AND BE PRESENT, IN THE NOW. BREATHE.
- [ ] **EXERCISE** – DID YOU MOVE AT LEAST 30 MINUTES TODAY?
- [ ] **FUEL** – EAT 80% NUTRIENT DENSE FOOD THAT ENERGIZES YOU

I WAS MOST GRATEFUL FOR TODAY

Good Evening Gorgeous!

I LOVE TO GIVE. TODAY I GAVE

CHEERS TO ME!!!
LET'S CELEBRATE MY SUCCESSES FOR THE DAY

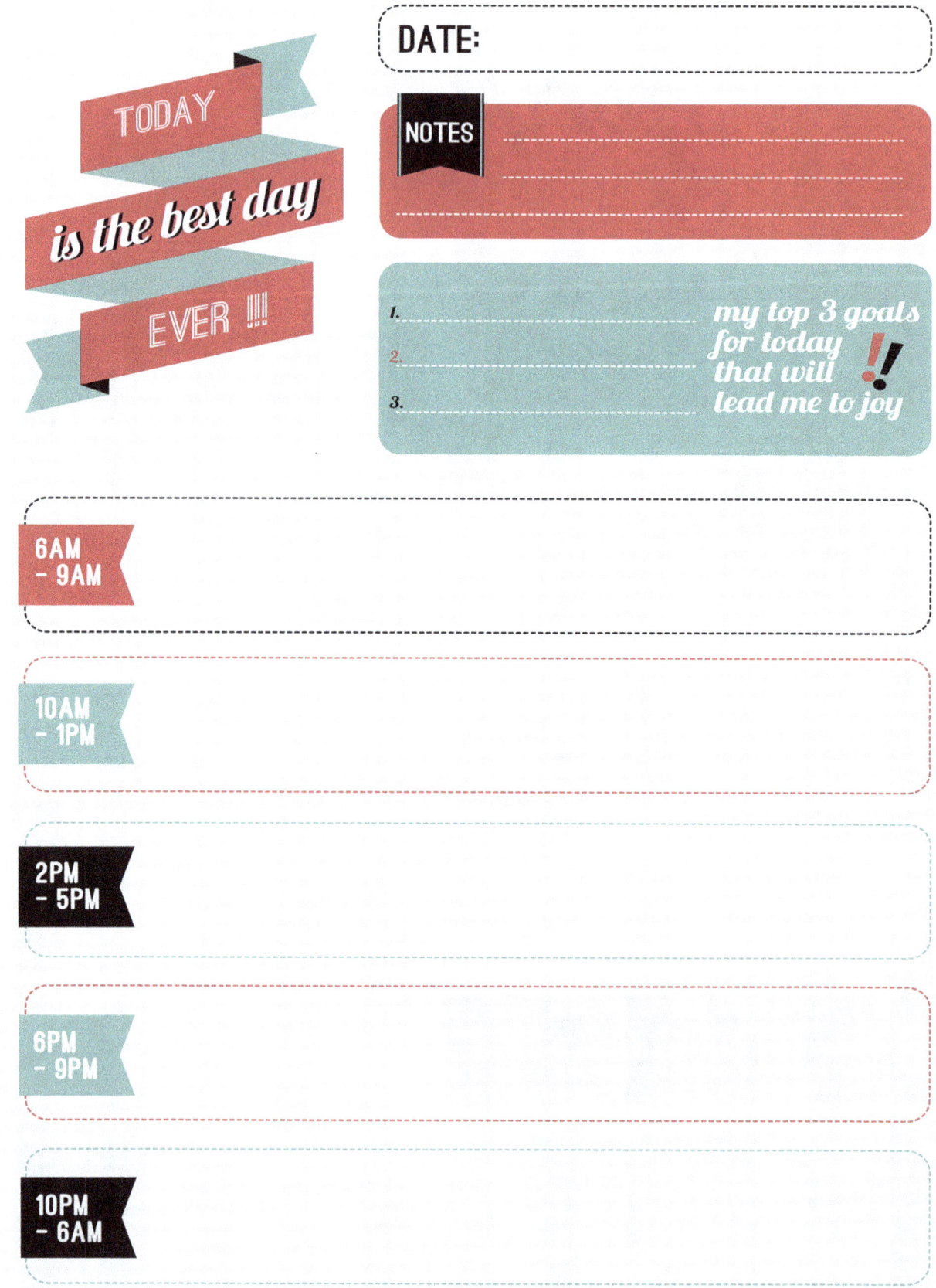

I AM BRILLIANT
gorgeous
TALENTED AND FABULOUS

GOOD MORNING gorgeous!

I AM GRATEFUL FOR

MY MANTRA *for today!*

FUN!!! TODAY FOR FUN I WILL

- [ ] VISUALIZATION – SET YOUR TIMER FOR A MINIMUM OF 5 MINUTES AND GO THERE!
- [ ] MEDITATION – SET YOUR TIMER FOR A MINIMUM OF 5 MINUTES AND BE PRESENT, IN THE NOW. BREATHE.
- [ ] EXERCISE – DID YOU MOVE AT LEAST 30 MINUTES TODAY?
- [ ] FUEL – EAT 80% NUTRIENT DENSE FOOD THAT ENERGIZES YOU

I WAS MOST GRATEFUL FOR TODAY

Good Evening Gorgeous!

I LOVE TO GIVE. TODAY I GAVE

CHEERS TO ME!!!
LET'S CELEBRATE MY SUCCESSES FOR THE DAY

I AM BRILLIANT
gorgeous
TALENTED AND FABULOUS

GOOD MORNING gorgeous!

I AM GRATEFUL FOR

MY MANTRA

for today!

FUN!!! TODAY FOR FUN I WILL

☐ VISUALIZATION – SET YOUR TIMER FOR A MINIMUM OF 5 MINUTES AND GO THERE!

☐ MEDITATION – SET YOUR TIMER FOR A MINIMUM OF 5 MINUTES AND BE PRESENT, IN THE NOW. BREATHE.

☐ EXERCISE – DID YOU MOVE AT LEAST 30 MINUTES TODAY?

☐ FUEL – EAT 80% NUTRIENT DENSE FOOD THAT ENERGIZES YOU

I WAS MOST GRATEFUL FOR TODAY

Good Evening Gorgeous!

I LOVE TO GIVE. TODAY I GAVE

CHEERS TO ME!!!
LET'S CELEBRATE MY SUCCESSES FOR THE DAY

I AM BRILLIANT
gorgeous
TALENTED AND FABULOUS

GOOD MORNING gorgeous!

MY MANTRA for today!
....
....
....
....

I AM GRATEFUL FOR
....
....
....

FUN!!! TODAY FOR FUN I WILL
....
....
....

- ☐ **VISUALIZATION** – SET YOUR TIMER FOR A MINIMUM OF 5 MINUTES AND GO THERE!
- ☐ **MEDITATION** – SET YOUR TIMER FOR A MINIMUM OF 5 MINUTES AND BE PRESENT, IN THE NOW. BREATHE.
- ☐ **EXERCISE** – DID YOU MOVE AT LEAST 30 MINUTES TODAY?
- ☐ **FUEL** – EAT 80% NUTRIENT DENSE FOOD THAT ENERGIZES YOU

I WAS MOST GRATEFUL FOR TODAY
....
....
....
....
....
....

Good Evening Gorgeous!

I LOVE TO GIVE. TODAY I GAVE
....
....
....

CHEERS TO ME!!!
LET'S CELEBRATE MY SUCCESSES FOR THE DAY
....
....
....

PAUSE CAFÉ
coffee break ;;

time to pause and reflect. are you focused on your goals? need to revise your priorities? get more specific with your visualization? add some new mantras? grab a cup of hot coffee or tea and sit down and focus on your joyful plan for the next 30 days.

L'ART DE VIVRE!
VISUALIZE THE NEXT 30 DAYS

RAISON D'ÊTRE!
WHAT ARE YOUR TOP 2-3 PRIORITIES?

PAIN AU CHOCOLAT
FOR YOUR BRAIN!
MANTRAS AND AFFIRMATIONS YOU NEED TO HEAR DAILY

LA VIE EST BELLE!
WHAT ARE YOU MOST GRATEFUL FOR FROM THE LAST 30 DAYS?

VIVRE LA VIE PAR LA CONCEPTION!
REVISIT YOUR 10 GOALS FOR THE YEAR
(THINGS CHANGE. PERSPECTIVE, PRIORITIES OR MAYBE YOU ACCOMPLISHED A GOAL AND WOULD LIKE TO ADD ANOTHER. OR, MAYBE THEY ARE THE SAME AND YOU NEED TO REWRITE THEM HERE)

GOOD MORNING gorgeous!

I AM GRATEFUL FOR
_____
_____
_____

MY MANTRA for today!
_____
_____
_____
_____

FUN!!! TODAY FOR FUN I WILL
_____
_____
_____

- ☐ VISUALIZATION – SET YOUR TIMER FOR A MINIMUM OF 5 MINUTES AND GO THERE!
- ☐ MEDITATION – SET YOUR TIMER FOR A MINIMUM OF 5 MINUTES AND BE PRESENT, IN THE NOW. BREATHE.
- ☐ EXERCISE – DID YOU MOVE AT LEAST 30 MINUTES TODAY?
- ☐ FUEL – EAT 80% NUTRIENT DENSE FOOD THAT ENERGIZES YOU

I WAS MOST GRATEFUL FOR TODAY
_____
_____
_____
_____
_____
_____

Good Evening Gorgeous!

I LOVE TO GIVE. TODAY I GAVE
_____
_____
_____

CHEERS TO ME!!!
LET'S CELEBRATE MY SUCCESSES FOR THE DAY
_____
_____
_____

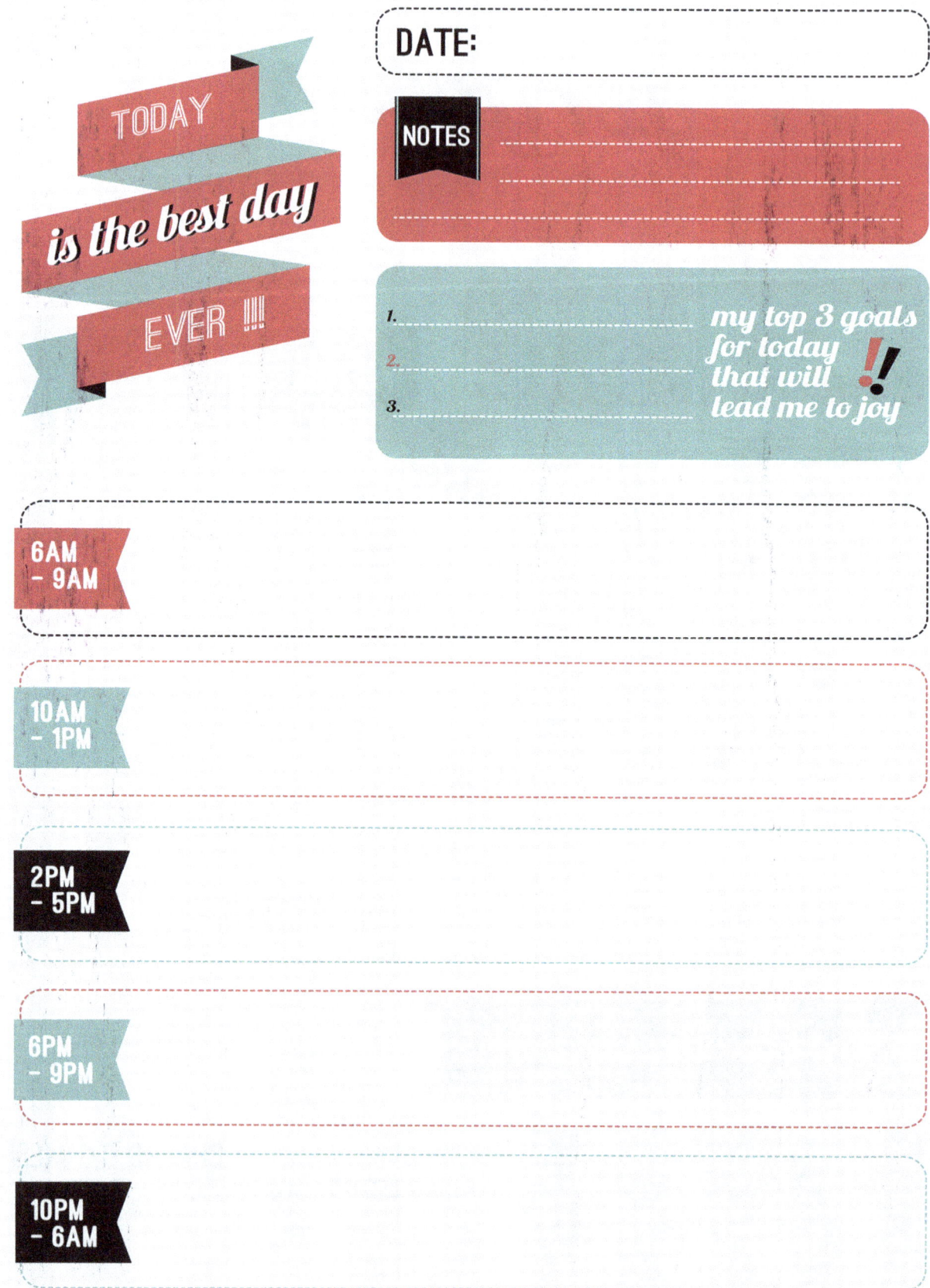

I AM BRILLIANT
gorgeous
TALENTED AND FABULOUS

GOOD MORNING gorgeous!

I AM GRATEFUL FOR

MY MANTRA for today!

FUN!!! TODAY FOR FUN I WILL

- ☐ VISUALIZATION – SET YOUR TIMER FOR A MINIMUM OF 5 MINUTES AND GO THERE!
- ☐ MEDITATION – SET YOUR TIMER FOR A MINIMUM OF 5 MINUTES AND BE PRESENT, IN THE NOW, BREATHE.
- ☐ EXERCISE – DID YOU MOVE AT LEAST 30 MINUTES TODAY?
- ☐ FUEL – EAT 80% NUTRIENT DENSE FOOD THAT ENERGIZES YOU

I WAS MOST GRATEFUL FOR TODAY

Good Evening Gorgeous!

I LOVE TO GIVE. TODAY I GAVE

CHEERS TO ME!!!
LET'S CELEBRATE MY SUCCESSES FOR THE DAY

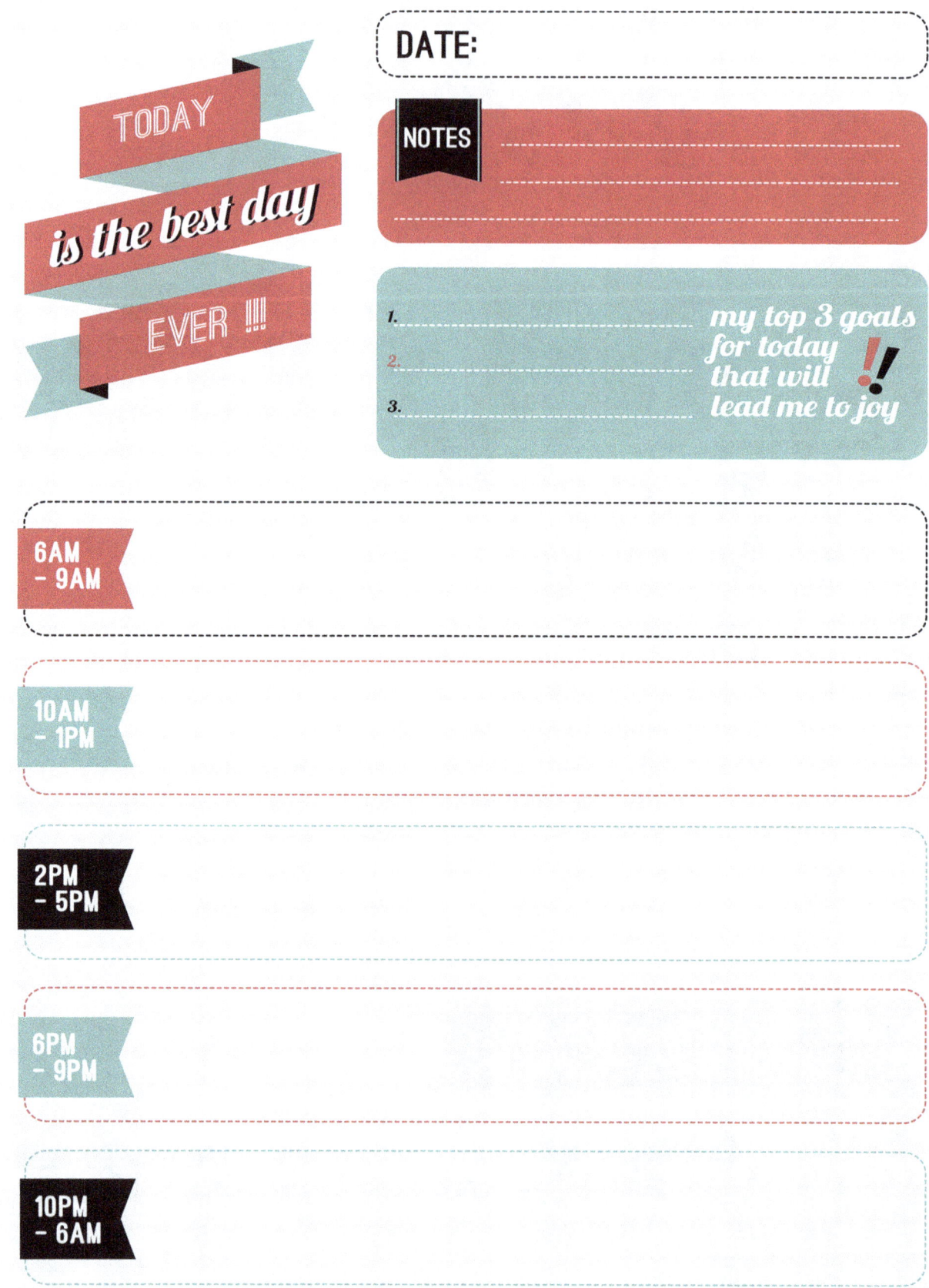

I AM BRILLIANT
gorgeous
TALENTED AND FABULOUS

GOOD MORNING gorgeous!

I AM GRATEFUL FOR
_____
_____
_____
_____

MY MANTRA for today!
_____
_____
_____
_____

FUN!!! TODAY FOR FUN I WILL
_____
_____
_____

☐ **VISUALIZATION** – SET YOUR TIMER FOR A MINIMUM OF 5 MINUTES AND GO THERE!

☐ **MEDITATION** – SET YOUR TIMER FOR A MINIMUM OF 5 MINUTES AND BE PRESENT, IN THE NOW. BREATHE.

☐ **EXERCISE** – DID YOU MOVE AT LEAST 30 MINUTES TODAY?

☐ **FUEL** – EAT 80% NUTRIENT DENSE FOOD THAT ENERGIZES YOU

I WAS MOST GRATEFUL FOR TODAY
_____
_____
_____
_____
_____
_____

Good Evening Gorgeous!

I LOVE TO GIVE. TODAY I GAVE
_____
_____
_____

CHEERS TO ME!!!
LET'S CELEBRATE MY SUCCESSES FOR THE DAY
_____
_____
_____

I AM BRILLIANT
gorgeous
TALENTED AND FABULOUS

GOOD MORNING gorgeous!

I AM GRATEFUL FOR

_____
_____
_____

 MY MANTRA  for today!

_____
_____
_____
_____

FUN!!! TODAY FOR FUN I WILL
_____
_____
_____

☐ **VISUALIZATION** – SET YOUR TIMER FOR A MINIMUM OF 5 MINUTES AND GO THERE!

☐ **MEDITATION** – SET YOUR TIMER FOR A MINIMUM OF 5 MINUTES AND BE PRESENT, IN THE NOW. BREATHE.

☐ **EXERCISE** – DID YOU MOVE AT LEAST 30 MINUTES TODAY?

☐ **FUEL** – EAT 80% NUTRIENT DENSE FOOD THAT ENERGIZES YOU

I WAS MOST GRATEFUL FOR TODAY
_____
_____
_____
_____
_____
_____

Good Evening Gorgeous!

I LOVE TO GIVE. TODAY I GAVE
_____
_____
_____

CHEERS TO ME!!!
LET'S CELEBRATE MY SUCCESSES FOR THE DAY
_____
_____
_____
_____

I AM BRILLIANT
gorgeous
TALENTED AND FABULOUS

GOOD MORNING gorgeous!

I AM GRATEFUL FOR

MY MANTRA *for today!*

FUN!!! TODAY FOR FUN I WILL

- [ ] VISUALIZATION – SET YOUR TIMER FOR A MINIMUM OF 5 MINUTES AND GO THERE!
- [ ] MEDITATION – SET YOUR TIMER FOR A MINIMUM OF 5 MINUTES AND BE PRESENT, IN THE NOW. BREATHE.
- [ ] EXERCISE – DID YOU MOVE AT LEAST 30 MINUTES TODAY?
- [ ] FUEL – EAT 80% NUTRIENT DENSE FOOD THAT ENERGIZES YOU

I WAS MOST GRATEFUL FOR TODAY

Good Evening Gorgeous!

I LOVE TO GIVE. TODAY I GAVE

CHEERS TO ME!!!
LET'S CELEBRATE MY SUCCESSES FOR THE DAY

I AM BRILLIANT
gorgeous
TALENTED AND FABULOUS

GOOD MORNING gorgeous!

I AM GRATEFUL FOR
_____
_____
_____

MY MANTRA *for today!*
_____
_____
_____
_____

FUN!!! TODAY FOR FUN I WILL
_____
_____
_____

- ☐ **VISUALIZATION** – SET YOUR TIMER FOR A MINIMUM OF 5 MINUTES AND GO THERE!
- ☐ **MEDITATION** – SET YOUR TIMER FOR A MINIMUM OF 5 MINUTES AND BE PRESENT, IN THE NOW. BREATHE.
- ☐ **EXERCISE** – DID YOU MOVE AT LEAST 30 MINUTES TODAY?
- ☐ **FUEL** – EAT 80% NUTRIENT DENSE FOOD THAT ENERGIZES YOU

I WAS MOST GRATEFUL FOR TODAY
_____
_____
_____
_____
_____

Good Evening Gorgeous!

I LOVE TO GIVE. TODAY I GAVE
_____
_____
_____

CHEERS TO ME!!!
LET'S CELEBRATE MY SUCCESSES FOR THE DAY
_____
_____
_____

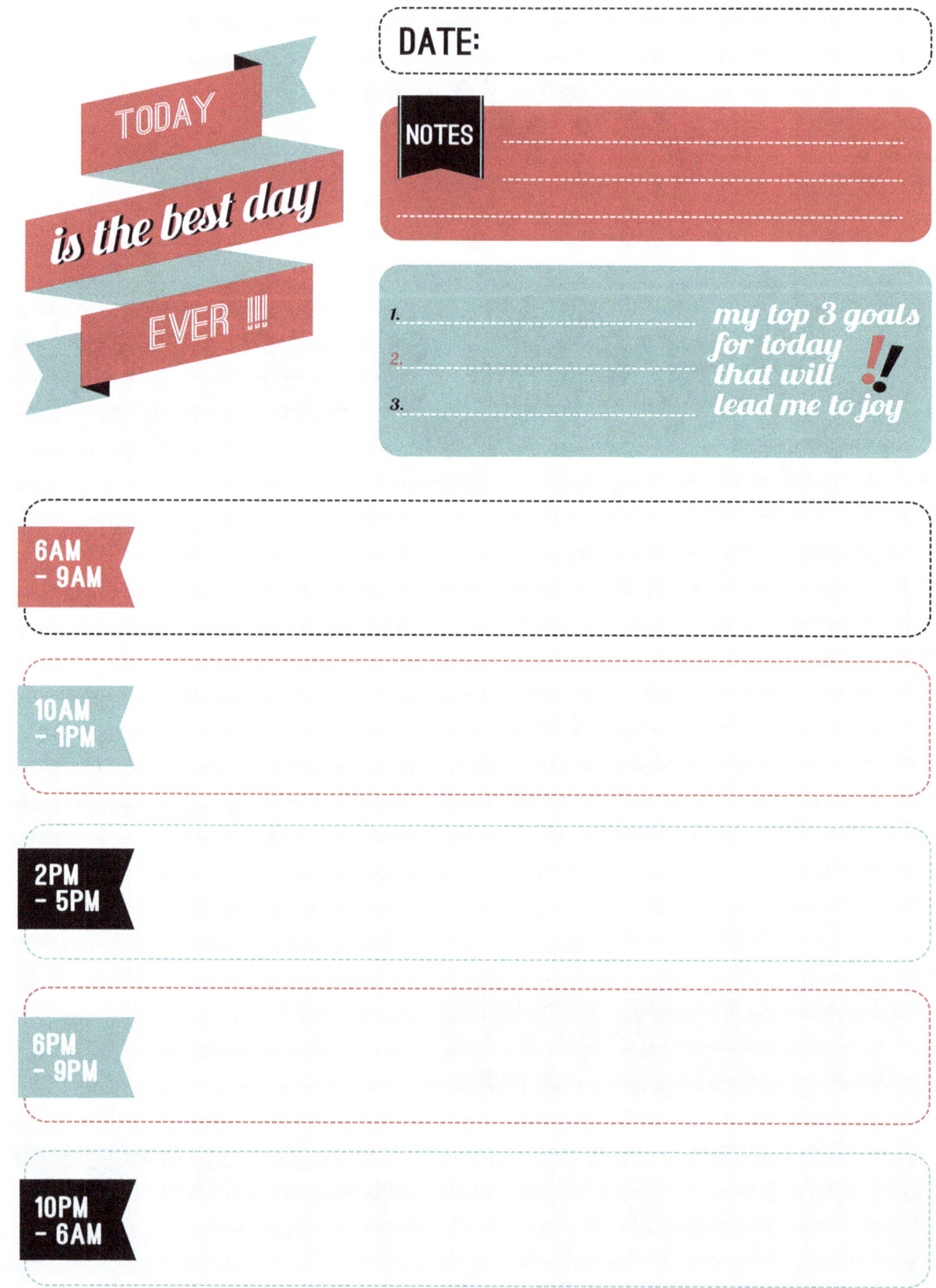

I AM BRILLIANT
gorgeous
TALENTED AND FABULOUS

GOOD MORNING gorgeous!

I AM GRATEFUL FOR

MY MANTRA for today!

FUN!!! TODAY FOR FUN I WILL

- ☐ **VISUALIZATION** – SET YOUR TIMER FOR A MINIMUM OF 5 MINUTES AND GO THERE!
- ☐ **MEDITATION** – SET YOUR TIMER FOR A MINIMUM OF 5 MINUTES AND BE PRESENT, IN THE NOW. BREATHE.
- ☐ **EXERCISE** – DID YOU MOVE AT LEAST 30 MINUTES TODAY?
- ☐ **FUEL** – EAT 80% NUTRIENT DENSE FOOD THAT ENERGIZES YOU

I WAS MOST GRATEFUL FOR TODAY

Good Evening Gorgeous!

I LOVE TO GIVE. TODAY I GAVE

CHEERS TO ME!!!
LET'S CELEBRATE MY SUCCESSES FOR THE DAY

I AM BRILLIANT
gorgeous
TALENTED AND FABULOUS

GOOD MORNING gorgeous!

I AM GRATEFUL FOR

MY MANTRA  for today!

FUN!!! TODAY FOR FUN I WILL

- [ ] VISUALIZATION - SET YOUR TIMER FOR A MINIMUM OF 5 MINUTES AND GO THERE!
- [ ] MEDITATION - SET YOUR TIMER FOR A MINIMUM OF 5 MINUTES AND BE PRESENT, IN THE NOW. BREATHE.
- [ ] EXERCISE - DID YOU MOVE AT LEAST 30 MINUTES TODAY?
- [ ] FUEL - EAT 80% NUTRIENT DENSE FOOD THAT ENERGIZES YOU

I WAS MOST GRATEFUL FOR TODAY

Good Evening Gorgeous!

I LOVE TO GIVE. TODAY I GAVE

CHEERS TO ME!!!
LET'S CELEBRATE MY SUCCESSES FOR THE DAY

I AM BRILLIANT
gorgeous
TALENTED AND FABULOUS

GOOD MORNING gorgeous!

I AM GRATEFUL FOR
....
....
....

MY MANTRA for today!
....
....
....

FUN!!! TODAY FOR FUN I WILL
....
....
....

- ☐ **VISUALIZATION** – SET YOUR TIMER FOR A MINIMUM OF 5 MINUTES AND GO THERE!
- ☐ **MEDITATION** – SET YOUR TIMER FOR A MINIMUM OF 5 MINUTES AND BE PRESENT, IN THE NOW. BREATHE.
- ☐ **EXERCISE** – DID YOU MOVE AT LEAST 30 MINUTES TODAY?
- ☐ **FUEL** – EAT 80% NUTRIENT DENSE FOOD THAT ENERGIZES YOU

I WAS MOST GRATEFUL FOR TODAY
....
....
....
....
....

Good Evening Gorgeous!

I LOVE TO GIVE. TODAY I GAVE
....
....
....

CHEERS TO ME!!!
LET'S CELEBRATE MY SUCCESSES FOR THE DAY
....
....
....

I AM BRILLIANT
gorgeous
TALENTED AND FABULOUS

GOOD MORNING gorgeous!

I AM GRATEFUL FOR

MY MANTRA for today!

FUN!!! TODAY FOR FUN I WILL

- ☐ **VISUALIZATION** – SET YOUR TIMER FOR A MINIMUM OF 5 MINUTES AND GO THERE!
- ☐ **MEDITATION** – SET YOUR TIMER FOR A MINIMUM OF 5 MINUTES AND BE PRESENT, IN THE NOW. BREATHE.
- ☐ **EXERCISE** – DID YOU MOVE AT LEAST 30 MINUTES TODAY?
- ☐ **FUEL** – EAT 80% NUTRIENT DENSE FOOD THAT ENERGIZES YOU

I WAS MOST GRATEFUL FOR TODAY

Good Evening Gorgeous!

I LOVE TO GIVE. TODAY I GAVE

CHEERS TO ME!!!
LET'S CELEBRATE MY SUCCESSES FOR THE DAY

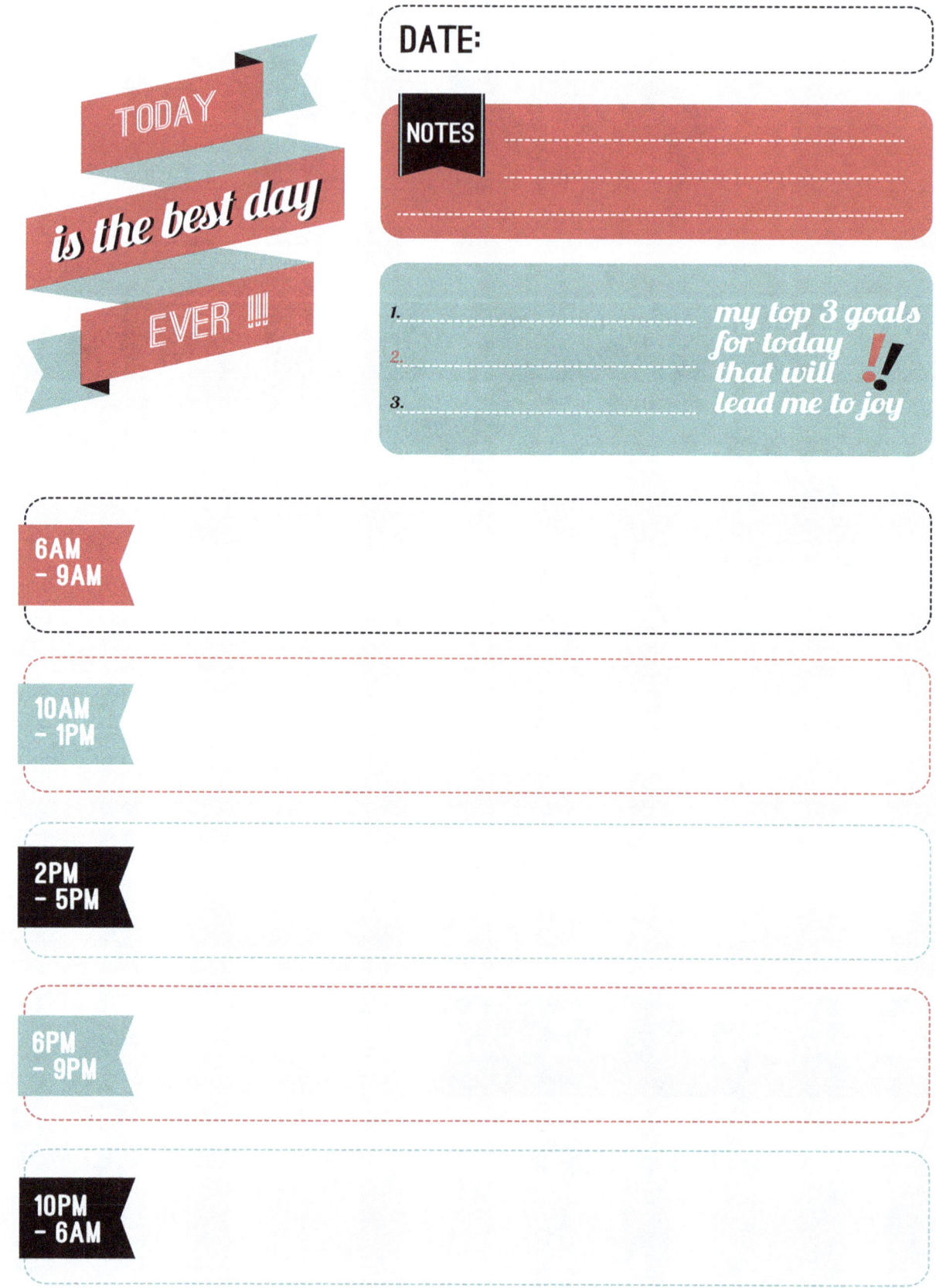

I AM GRATEFUL FOR

MY MANTRA

FUN!!! TODAY FOR FUN I WILL

- VISUALIZATION – SET YOUR TIMER FOR A MINIMUM OF 5 MINUTES AND GO THERE!
- MEDITATION – SET YOUR TIMER FOR A MINIMUM OF 5 MINUTES AND BE PRESENT, IN THE NOW. BREATHE.
- EXERCISE – DID YOU MOVE AT LEAST 30 MINUTES TODAY?
- FUEL – EAT 80% NUTRIENT DENSE FOOD THAT ENERGIZES YOU

I WAS MOST GRATEFUL FOR TODAY

Good Evening Gorgeous!

I LOVE TO GIVE. TODAY I GAVE

CHEERS TO ME!!!
LET'S CELEBRATE MY SUCCESSES FOR THE DAY

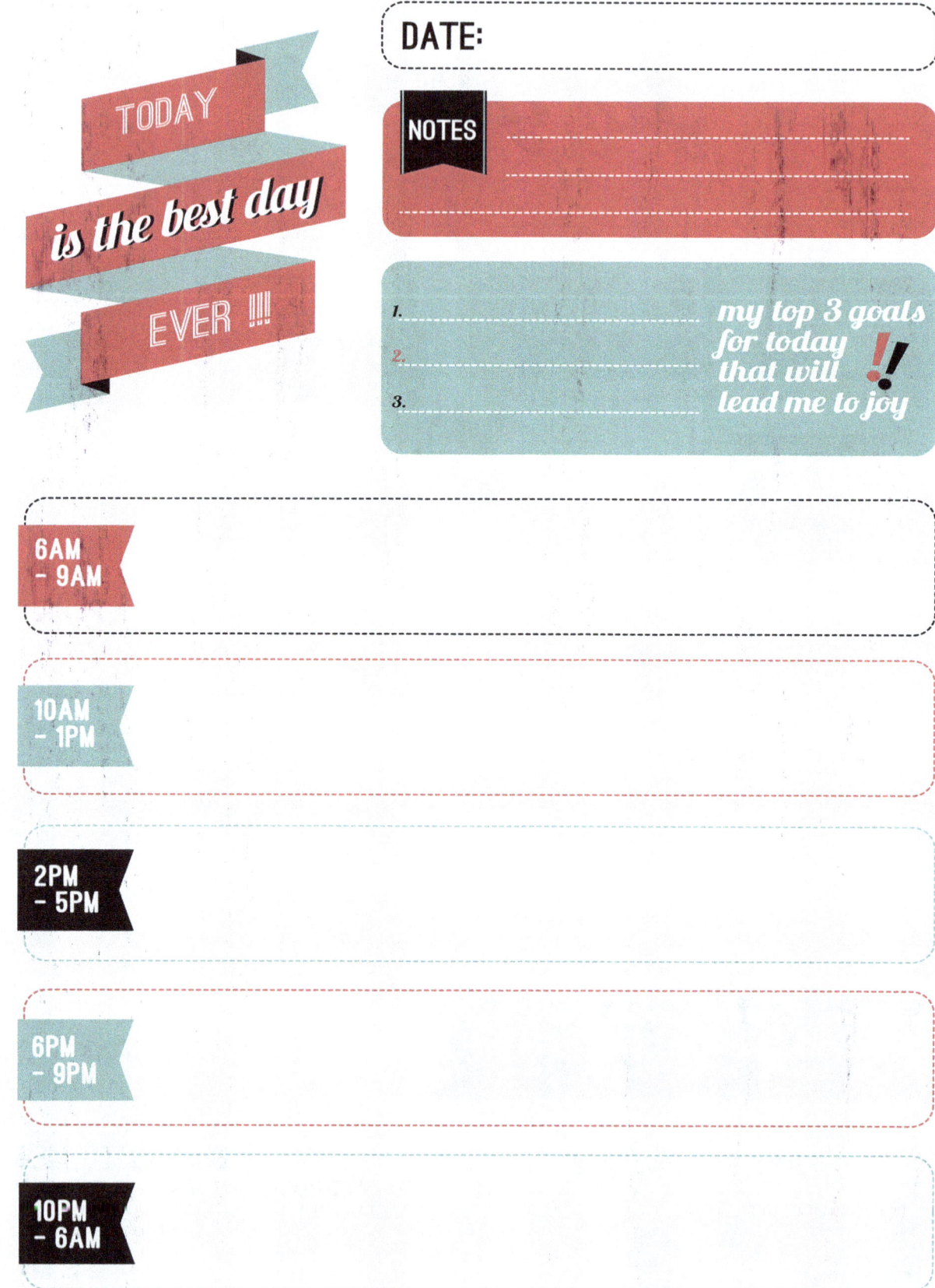

I AM BRILLIANT
gorgeous
TALENTED AND FABULOUS

GOOD MORNING gorgeous!

I AM GRATEFUL FOR
....
....
....

MY MANTRA *for today!*
....
....
....

FUN!!! TODAY FOR FUN I WILL
....
....
....

☐ VISUALIZATION – SET YOUR TIMER FOR A MINIMUM OF 5 MINUTES AND GO THERE!
☐ MEDITATION – SET YOUR TIMER FOR A MINIMUM OF 5 MINUTES AND BE PRESENT, IN THE NOW. BREATHE.
☐ EXERCISE – DID YOU MOVE AT LEAST 30 MINUTES TODAY?
☐ FUEL – EAT 80% NUTRIENT DENSE FOOD THAT ENERGIZES YOU

I WAS MOST GRATEFUL FOR TODAY
....
....
....
....
....
....

Good Evening Gorgeous!

I LOVE TO GIVE. TODAY I GAVE
....
....
....

CHEERS TO ME!!!
LET'S CELEBRATE MY SUCCESSES FOR THE DAY
....
....
....

I AM BRILLIANT
gorgeous
TALENTED AND FABULOUS

GOOD MORNING gorgeous!

I AM GRATEFUL FOR
_____
_____
_____
_____

MY MANTRA *for today!*
_____
_____
_____
_____

FUN!!! TODAY FOR FUN I WILL
_____
_____
_____

☐ VISUALIZATION – SET YOUR TIMER FOR A MINIMUM OF 5 MINUTES AND GO THERE!
☐ MEDITATION – SET YOUR TIMER FOR A MINIMUM OF 5 MINUTES AND BE PRESENT, IN THE NOW. BREATHE.
☐ EXERCISE – DID YOU MOVE AT LEAST 30 MINUTES TODAY?
☐ FUEL – EAT 80% NUTRIENT DENSE FOOD THAT ENERGIZES YOU

I WAS MOST GRATEFUL FOR TODAY
_____
_____
_____
_____
_____

Good Evening Gorgeous!

I LOVE TO GIVE. TODAY I GAVE
_____
_____
_____

CHEERS TO ME!!!
LET'S CELEBRATE MY SUCCESSES FOR THE DAY
_____
_____
_____

I AM BRILLIANT
gorgeous
TALENTED AND FABULOUS

GOOD MORNING gorgeous!

I AM GRATEFUL FOR
....
....
....

MY MANTRA for today!
....
....
....
....

FUN!!! TODAY FOR FUN I WILL
....
....
....

- ☐ **VISUALIZATION** – SET YOUR TIMER FOR A MINIMUM OF 5 MINUTES AND GO THERE!
- ☐ **MEDITATION** – SET YOUR TIMER FOR A MINIMUM OF 5 MINUTES AND BE PRESENT, IN THE NOW. BREATHE.
- ☐ **EXERCISE** – DID YOU MOVE AT LEAST 30 MINUTES TODAY?
- ☐ **FUEL** – EAT 80% NUTRIENT DENSE FOOD THAT ENERGIZES YOU

I WAS MOST GRATEFUL FOR TODAY
....
....
....
....
....
....

Good Evening Gorgeous!

I LOVE TO GIVE. TODAY I GAVE
....
....
....

CHEERS TO ME!!!
LET'S CELEBRATE MY SUCCESSES FOR THE DAY
....
....
....

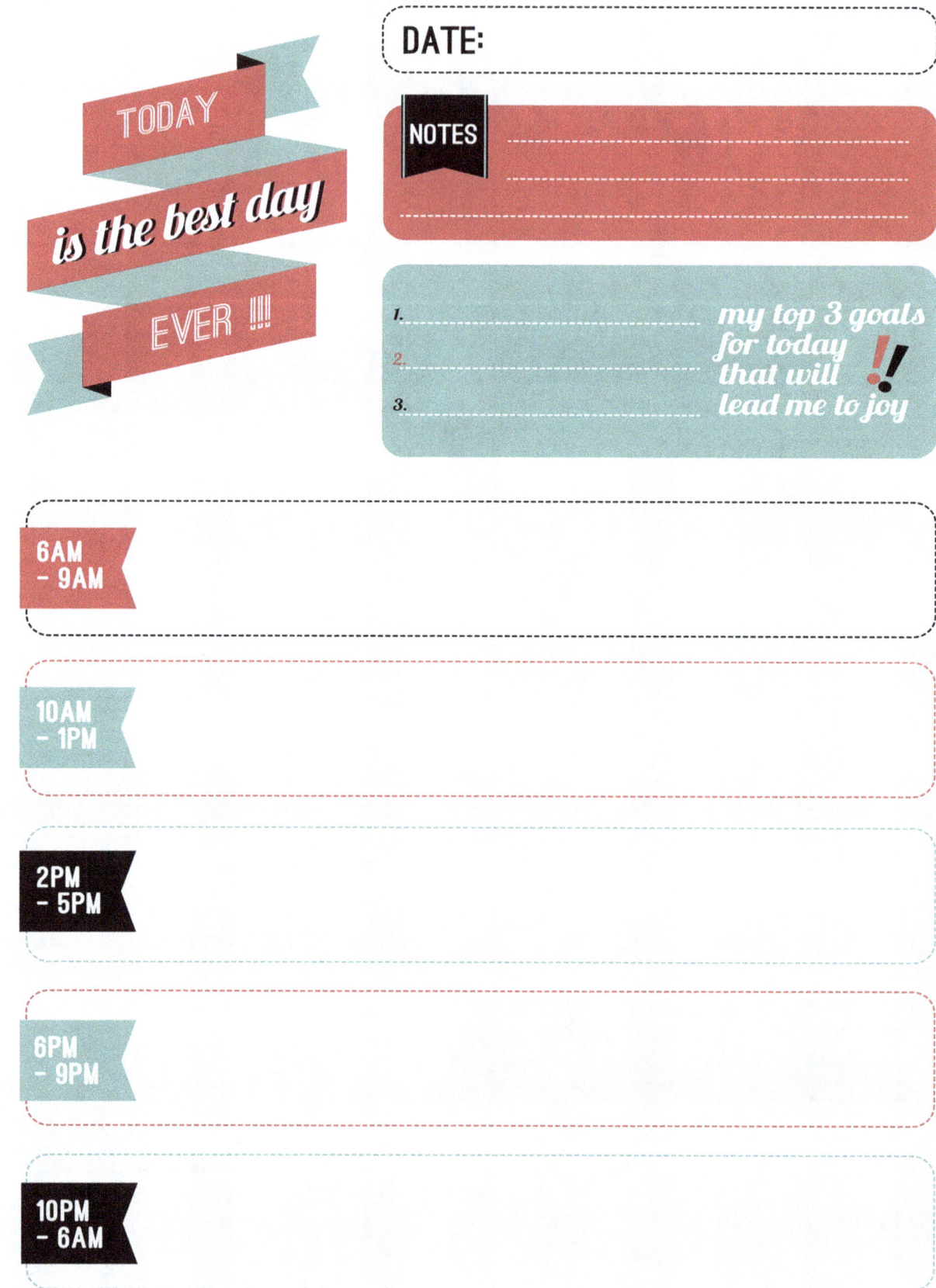

I AM BRILLIANT
gorgeous
TALENTED AND FABULOUS

GOOD MORNING gorgeous!

I AM GRATEFUL FOR

_____
_____

MY MANTRA for today!

_____
_____
_____

FUN!!! TODAY FOR FUN I WILL
_____
_____
_____

- ☐ **VISUALIZATION** – SET YOUR TIMER FOR A MINIMUM OF 5 MINUTES AND GO THERE!
- ☐ **MEDITATION** – SET YOUR TIMER FOR A MINIMUM OF 5 MINUTES AND BE PRESENT, IN THE NOW. BREATHE.
- ☐ **EXERCISE** – DID YOU MOVE AT LEAST 30 MINUTES TODAY?
- ☐ **FUEL** – EAT 80% NUTRIENT DENSE FOOD THAT ENERGIZES YOU

I WAS MOST GRATEFUL FOR TODAY
_____
_____
_____
_____
_____

Good Evening Gorgeous!

I LOVE TO GIVE. TODAY I GAVE
_____
_____
_____

CHEERS TO ME!!!
LET'S CELEBRATE MY SUCCESSES FOR THE DAY
_____
_____
_____

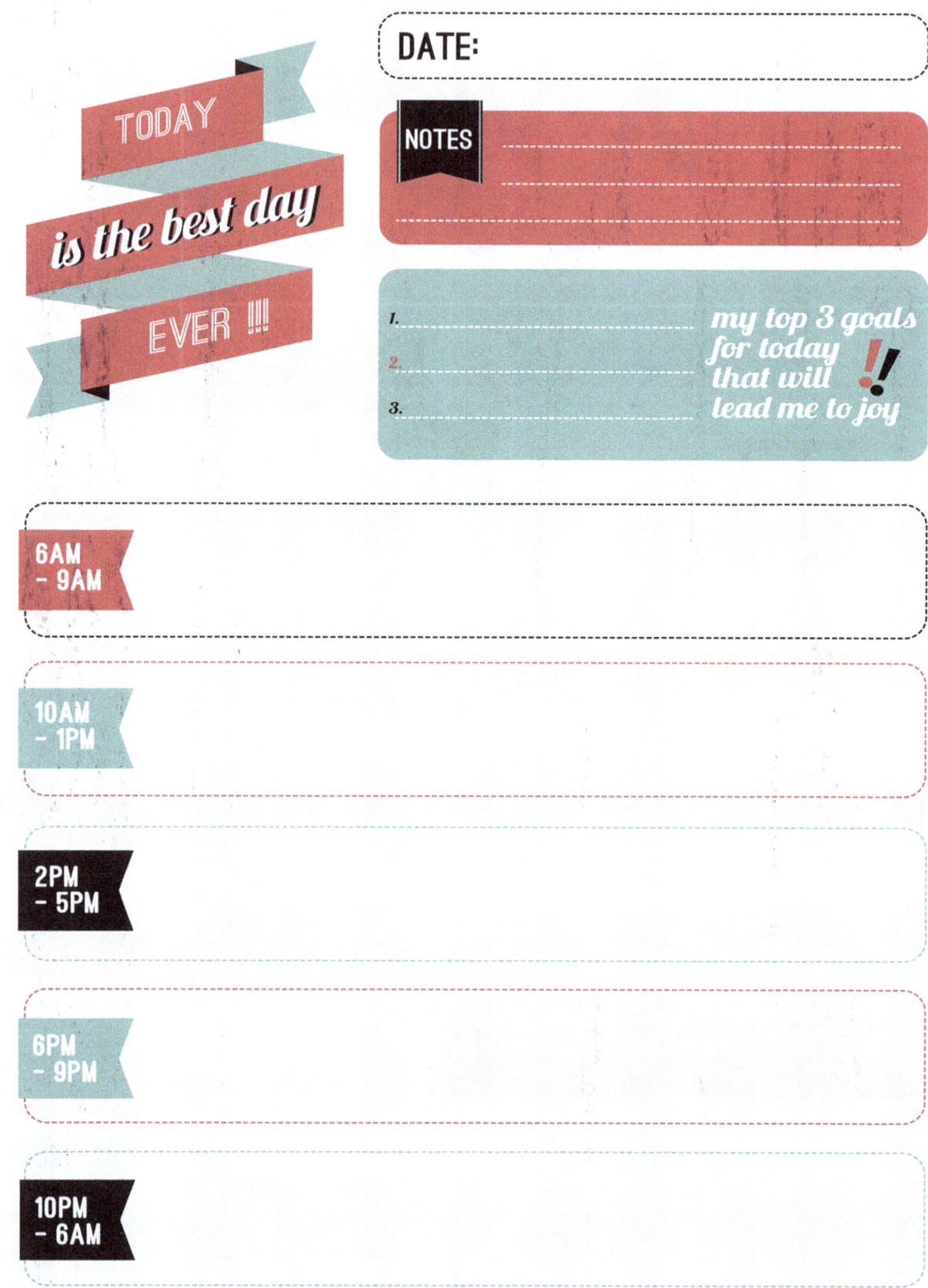

I AM BRILLIANT
gorgeous
TALENTED AND FABULOUS

GOOD MORNING *gorgeous!*

I AM GRATEFUL FOR

_____
_____
_____

MY MANTRA *for today!*

_____
_____
_____

FUN!!! TODAY FOR FUN I WILL

_____
_____
_____

- [ ] **VISUALIZATION** – SET YOUR TIMER FOR A MINIMUM OF 5 MINUTES AND GO THERE!
- [ ] **MEDITATION** – SET YOUR TIMER FOR A MINIMUM OF 5 MINUTES AND BE PRESENT, IN THE NOW. BREATHE.
- [ ] **EXERCISE** – DID YOU MOVE AT LEAST 30 MINUTES TODAY?
- [ ] **FUEL** – EAT 80% NUTRIENT DENSE FOOD THAT ENERGIZES YOU

I WAS MOST GRATEFUL FOR TODAY

_____
_____
_____
_____
_____
_____

Good Evening Gorgeous!

I LOVE TO GIVE. TODAY I GAVE

_____
_____
_____

CHEERS TO ME!!!
LET'S CELEBRATE MY SUCCESSES FOR THE DAY

_____
_____
_____

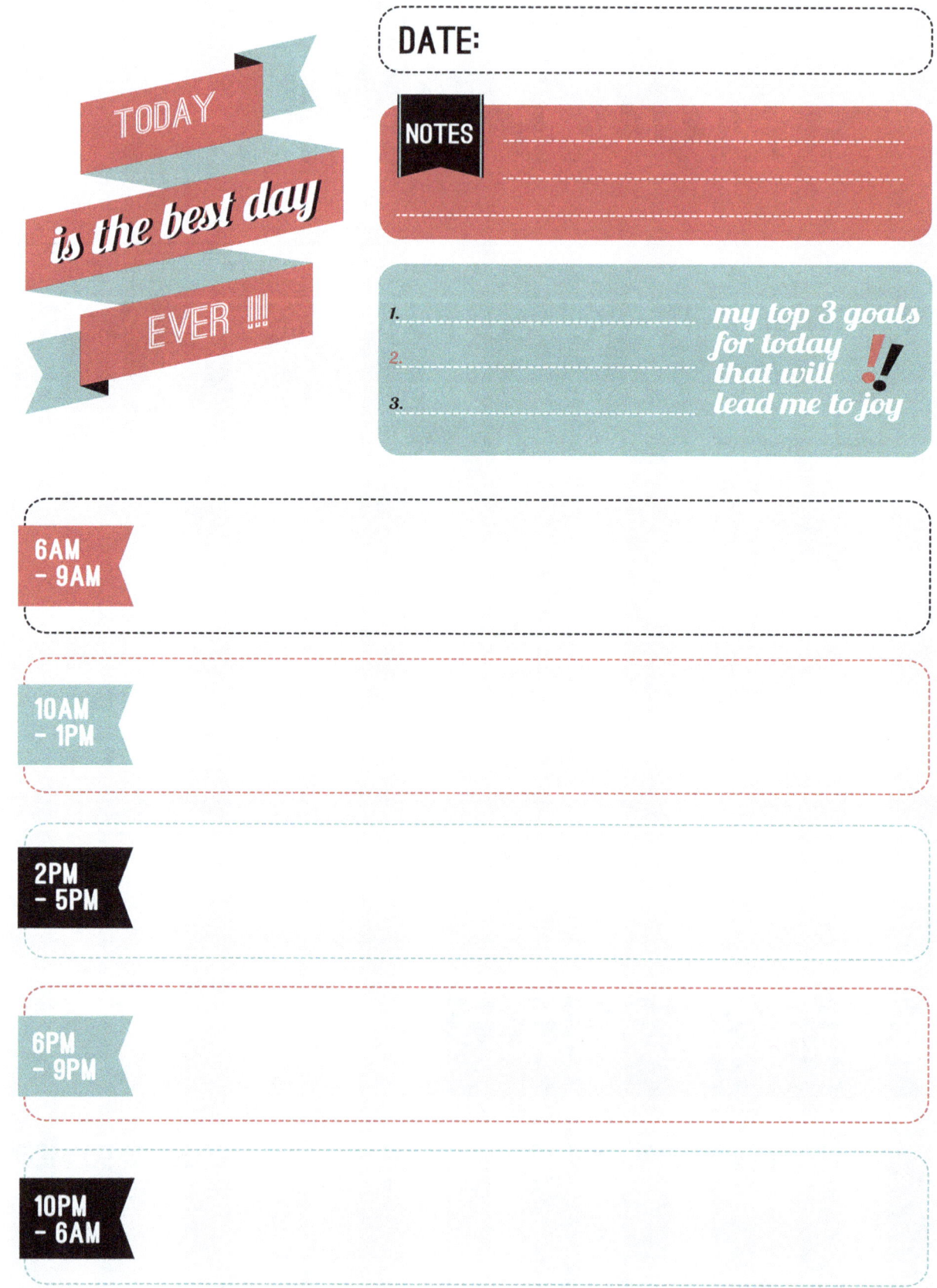

I AM BRILLIANT
gorgeous
TALENTED AND FABULOUS

GOOD MORNING gorgeous!

I AM GRATEFUL FOR
....
....
....
....

MY MANTRA for today!
....
....
....
....

FUN!!! TODAY FOR FUN I WILL
....
....
....

- ☐ **VISUALIZATION** – SET YOUR TIMER FOR A MINIMUM OF 5 MINUTES AND GO THERE!
- ☐ **MEDITATION** – SET YOUR TIMER FOR A MINIMUM OF 5 MINUTES AND BE PRESENT, IN THE NOW. BREATHE.
- ☐ **EXERCISE** – DID YOU MOVE AT LEAST 30 MINUTES TODAY?
- ☐ **FUEL** – EAT 80% NUTRIENT DENSE FOOD THAT ENERGIZES YOU

I WAS MOST GRATEFUL FOR TODAY
....
....
....
....
....

Good Evening Gorgeous!

I LOVE TO GIVE. TODAY I GAVE
....
....
....

CHEERS TO ME!!!
LET'S CELEBRATE MY SUCCESSES FOR THE DAY
....
....
....

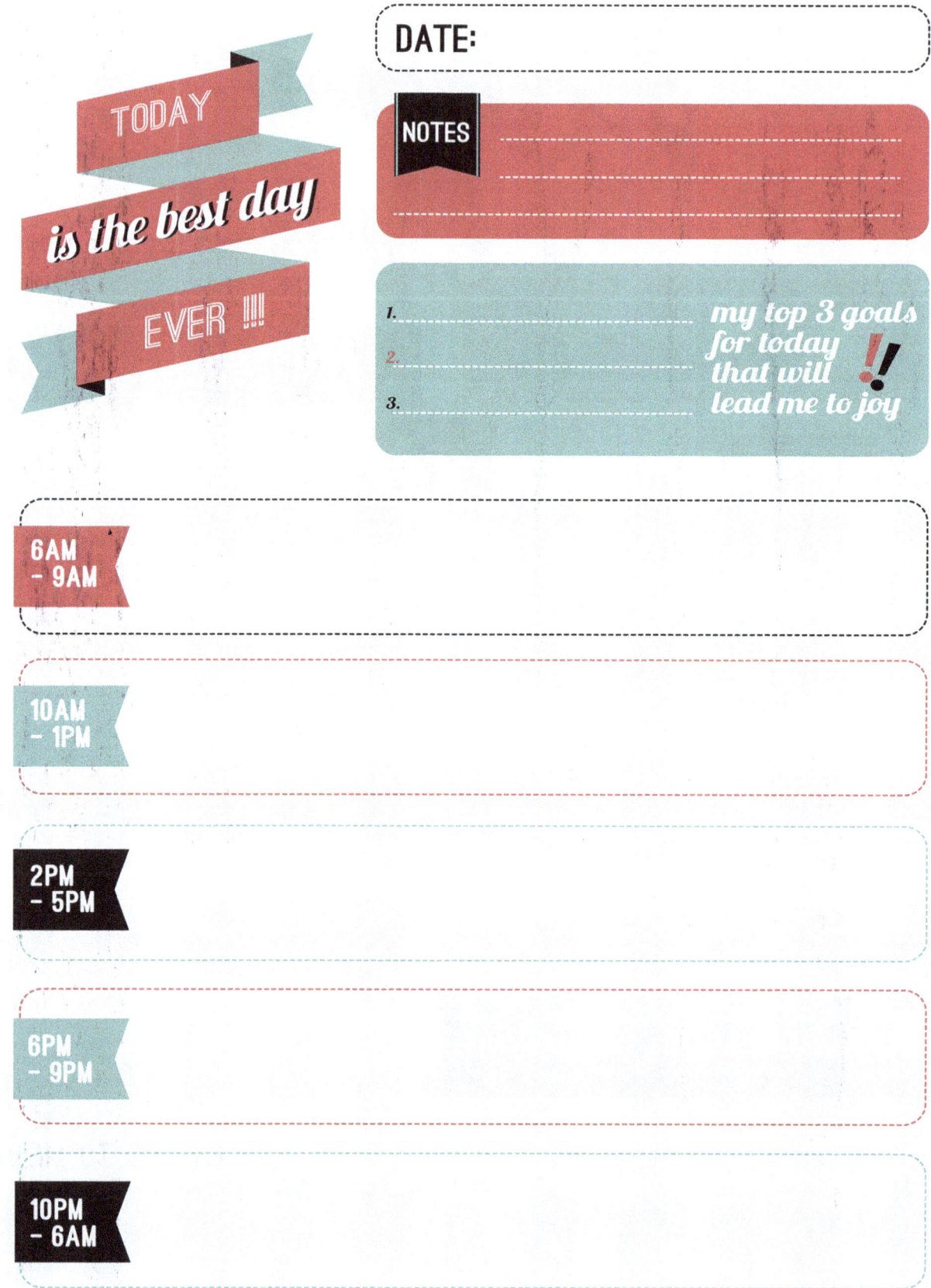

I AM BRILLIANT
gorgeous
TALENTED AND FABULOUS

GOOD MORNING gorgeous!

I AM GRATEFUL FOR

MY MANTRA *for today!*

FUN!!! TODAY FOR FUN I WILL

- [ ] **VISUALIZATION** – SET YOUR TIMER FOR A MINIMUM OF 5 MINUTES AND GO THERE!
- [ ] **MEDITATION** – SET YOUR TIMER FOR A MINIMUM OF 5 MINUTES AND BE PRESENT, IN THE NOW. BREATHE.
- [ ] **EXERCISE** – DID YOU MOVE AT LEAST 30 MINUTES TODAY?
- [ ] **FUEL** – EAT 80% NUTRIENT DENSE FOOD THAT ENERGIZES YOU

I WAS MOST GRATEFUL FOR TODAY

Good Evening Gorgeous!

I LOVE TO GIVE. TODAY I GAVE

CHEERS TO ME!!!
LET'S CELEBRATE MY SUCCESSES FOR THE DAY

I AM BRILLIANT
gorgeous
TALENTED AND FABULOUS

GOOD MORNING gorgeous!

I AM GRATEFUL FOR
_____
_____
_____

MY MANTRA for today!
_____
_____
_____
_____

FUN!!! TODAY FOR FUN I WILL
_____
_____
_____

- ☐ VISUALIZATION - SET YOUR TIMER FOR A MINIMUM OF 5 MINUTES AND GO THERE!
- ☐ MEDITATION - SET YOUR TIMER FOR A MINIMUM OF 5 MINUTES AND BE PRESENT, IN THE NOW. BREATHE.
- ☐ EXERCISE - DID YOU MOVE AT LEAST 30 MINUTES TODAY?
- ☐ FUEL - EAT 80% NUTRIENT DENSE FOOD THAT ENERGIZES YOU

I WAS MOST GRATEFUL FOR TODAY
_____
_____
_____
_____
_____

Good Evening Gorgeous!

I LOVE TO GIVE. TODAY I GAVE
_____
_____
_____

CHEERS TO ME!!!
LET'S CELEBRATE MY SUCCESSES FOR THE DAY
_____
_____
_____

I AM BRILLIANT
gorgeous
TALENTED AND FABULOUS

GOOD MORNING gorgeous!

I AM GRATEFUL FOR

 **MY MANTRA**  **for today!**

FUN!!! TODAY FOR FUN I WILL

☐ VISUALIZATION – SET YOUR TIMER FOR A MINIMUM OF 5 MINUTES AND GO THERE!

☐ MEDITATION – SET YOUR TIMER FOR A MINIMUM OF 5 MINUTES AND BE PRESENT, IN THE NOW. BREATHE.

☐ EXERCISE – DID YOU MOVE AT LEAST 30 MINUTES TODAY?

☐ FUEL – EAT 80% NUTRIENT DENSE FOOD THAT ENERGIZES YOU

I WAS MOST GRATEFUL FOR TODAY

Good Evening Gorgeous!

 **I LOVE TO GIVE. TODAY I GAVE**

CHEERS TO ME!!!
LET'S CELEBRATE MY SUCCESSES FOR THE DAY

I AM BRILLIANT
gorgeous
TALENTED AND FABULOUS

GOOD MORNING gorgeous!

I AM GRATEFUL FOR
_____
_____
_____
_____

MY MANTRA *for today!*
_____
_____
_____
_____

FUN!!! TODAY FOR FUN I WILL
_____
_____
_____

- ☐ **VISUALIZATION** – SET YOUR TIMER FOR A MINIMUM OF 5 MINUTES AND GO THERE!
- ☐ **MEDITATION** – SET YOUR TIMER FOR A MINIMUM OF 5 MINUTES AND BE PRESENT, IN THE NOW. BREATHE.
- ☐ **EXERCISE** – DID YOU MOVE AT LEAST 30 MINUTES TODAY?
- ☐ **FUEL** – EAT 80% NUTRIENT DENSE FOOD THAT ENERGIZES YOU

I WAS MOST GRATEFUL FOR TODAY
_____
_____
_____
_____
_____
_____

Good Evening Gorgeous!

I LOVE TO GIVE. TODAY I GAVE
_____
_____
_____
_____

CHEERS TO ME!!!
LET'S CELEBRATE MY SUCCESSES FOR THE DAY
_____
_____
_____

I AM BRILLIANT
gorgeous
TALENTED AND FABULOUS

GOOD MORNING *gorgeous!*

I AM GRATEFUL FOR
....
....
....

MY MANTRA *for today!*
....
....
....
....

FUN!!! TODAY FOR FUN I WILL
....
....
....

☐ **VISUALIZATION** – SET YOUR TIMER FOR A MINIMUM OF 5 MINUTES AND GO THERE!
☐ **MEDITATION** – SET YOUR TIMER FOR A MINIMUM OF 5 MINUTES AND BE PRESENT, IN THE NOW. BREATHE.
☐ **EXERCISE** – DID YOU MOVE AT LEAST 30 MINUTES TODAY?
☐ **FUEL** – EAT 80% NUTRIENT DENSE FOOD THAT ENERGIZES YOU

I WAS MOST GRATEFUL FOR TODAY
....
....
....
....
....

Good Evening Gorgeous!

I LOVE TO GIVE. TODAY I GAVE
....
....
....

CHEERS TO ME!!!
LET'S CELEBRATE MY SUCCESSES FOR THE DAY
....
....
....

I AM BRILLIANT
gorgeous
TALENTED AND FABULOUS

GOOD MORNING gorgeous!

I AM GRATEFUL FOR
_____
_____
_____
_____

MY MANTRA *for today!*
_____
_____
_____
_____

FUN!!! TODAY FOR FUN I WILL
_____
_____
_____

- ☐ VISUALIZATION – SET YOUR TIMER FOR A MINIMUM OF 5 MINUTES AND GO THERE!
- ☐ MEDITATION – SET YOUR TIMER FOR A MINIMUM OF 5 MINUTES AND BE PRESENT. IN THE NOW. BREATHE.
- ☐ EXERCISE – DID YOU MOVE AT LEAST 30 MINUTES TODAY?
- ☐ FUEL – EAT 80% NUTRIENT DENSE FOOD THAT ENERGIZES YOU

I WAS MOST GRATEFUL FOR TODAY
_____
_____
_____
_____
_____
_____
_____

Good Evening Gorgeous!

I LOVE TO GIVE. TODAY I GAVE
_____
_____
_____

CHEERS TO ME!!!
LET'S CELEBRATE MY SUCCESSES FOR THE DAY
_____
_____
_____

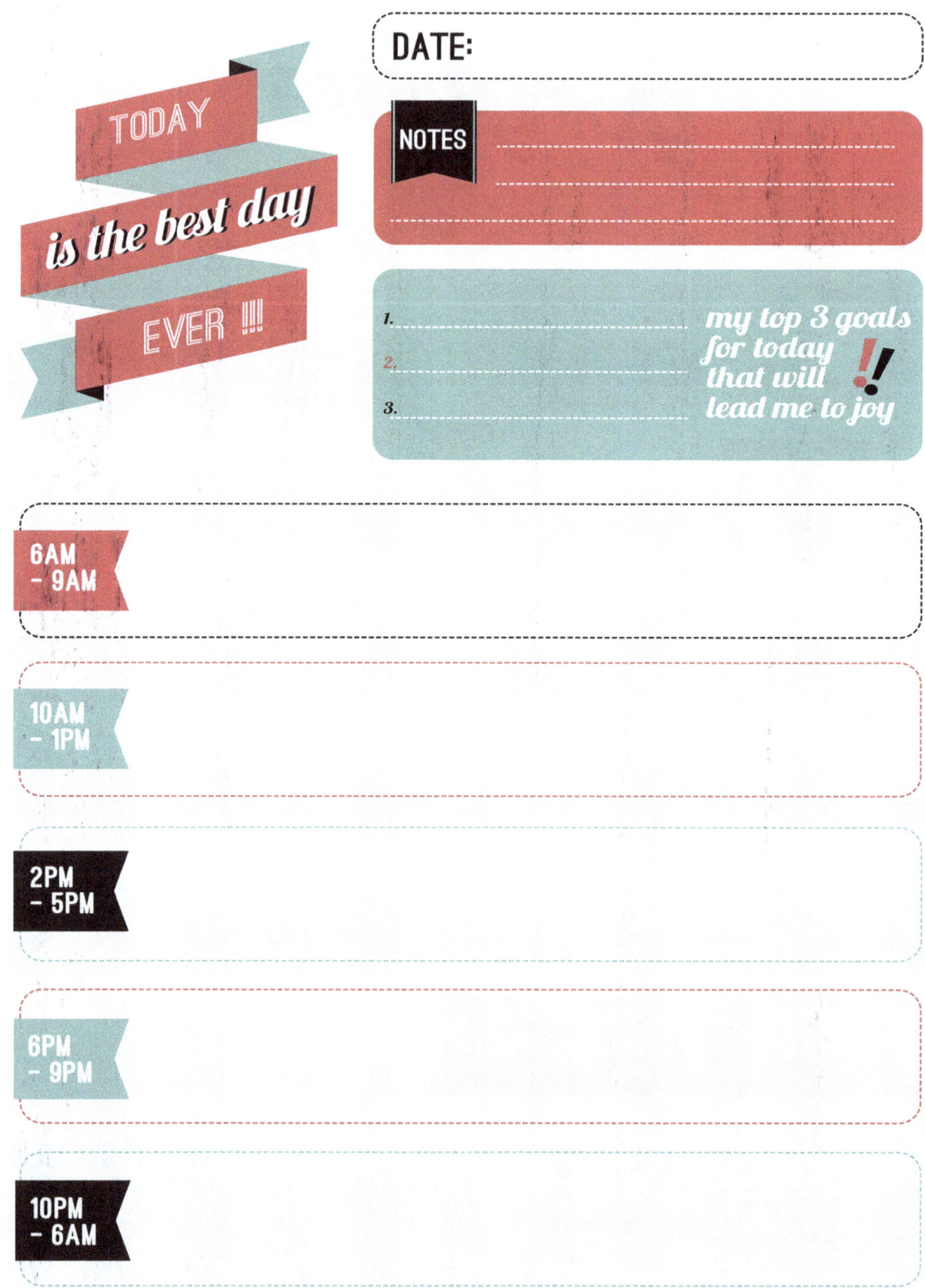

I AM BRILLIANT
gorgeous
TALENTED AND FABULOUS

GOOD MORNING gorgeous!

I AM GRATEFUL FOR

MY MANTRA *for today!*

FUN!!! TODAY FOR FUN I WILL

- ☐ **VISUALIZATION** – SET YOUR TIMER FOR A MINIMUM OF 5 MINUTES AND GO THERE!
- ☐ **MEDITATION** – SET YOUR TIMER FOR A MINIMUM OF 5 MINUTES AND BE PRESENT, IN THE NOW. BREATHE.
- ☐ **EXERCISE** – DID YOU MOVE AT LEAST 30 MINUTES TODAY?
- ☐ **FUEL** – EAT 80% NUTRIENT DENSE FOOD THAT ENERGIZES YOU

I WAS MOST GRATEFUL FOR TODAY

Good Evening Gorgeous!

I LOVE TO GIVE. TODAY I GAVE

CHEERS TO ME!!!
LET'S CELEBRATE MY SUCCESSES FOR THE DAY

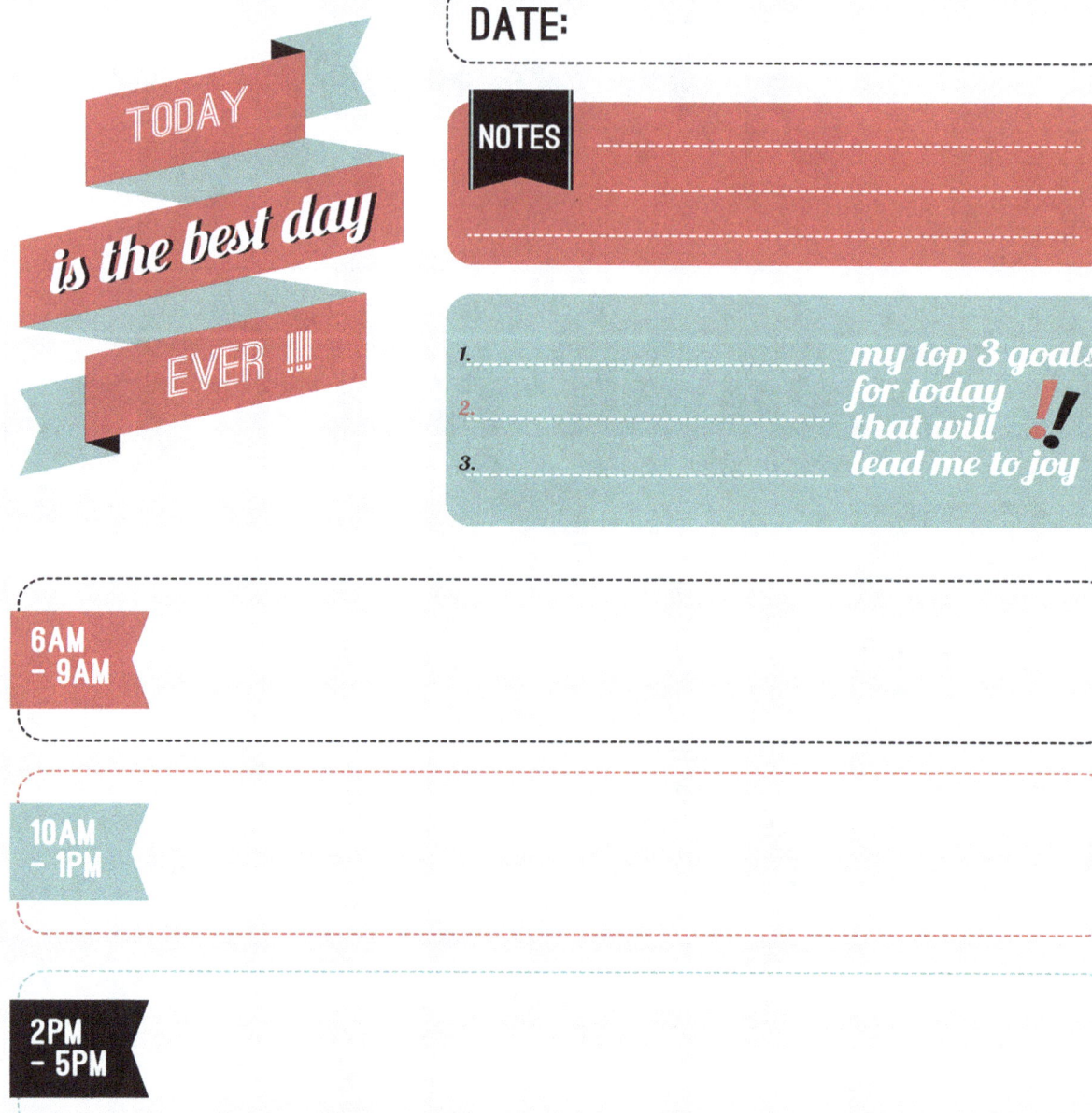

I AM BRILLIANT
gorgeous
TALENTED AND FABULOUS

I AM GRATEFUL FOR

FUN!!! TODAY FOR FUN I WILL

- ☐ VISUALIZATION – SET YOUR TIMER FOR A MINIMUM OF 5 MINUTES AND GO THERE!
- ☐ MEDITATION – SET YOUR TIMER FOR A MINIMUM OF 5 MINUTES AND BE PRESENT, IN THE NOW. BREATHE.
- ☐ EXERCISE – DID YOU MOVE AT LEAST 30 MINUTES TODAY?
- ☐ FUEL – EAT 80% NUTRIENT DENSE FOOD THAT ENERGIZES YOU

I WAS MOST GRATEFUL FOR TODAY

Good Evening Gorgeous!

I LOVE TO GIVE. TODAY I GAVE

CHEERS TO ME!!!
LET'S CELEBRATE MY SUCCESSES FOR THE DAY

I AM BRILLIANT
gorgeous
TALENTED AND FABULOUS

GOOD MORNING gorgeous!

I AM GRATEFUL FOR

MY MANTRA *for today!*

FUN!!! TODAY FOR FUN I WILL

☐ VISUALIZATION – SET YOUR TIMER FOR A MINIMUM OF 5 MINUTES AND GO THERE!

☐ MEDITATION – SET YOUR TIMER FOR A MINIMUM OF 5 MINUTES AND BE PRESENT, IN THE NOW. BREATHE.

☐ EXERCISE – DID YOU MOVE AT LEAST 30 MINUTES TODAY?

☐ FUEL – EAT 80% NUTRIENT DENSE FOOD THAT ENERGIZES YOU

I WAS MOST GRATEFUL FOR TODAY

Good Evening Gorgeous!

I LOVE TO GIVE. TODAY I GAVE

CHEERS TO ME!!!
LET'S CELEBRATE MY SUCCESSES FOR THE DAY

I AM BRILLIANT
gorgeous
TALENTED AND FABULOUS

GOOD MORNING gorgeous!

I AM GRATEFUL FOR

MY MANTRA *for today!*

FUN!!! TODAY FOR FUN I WILL

- ☐ VISUALIZATION – SET YOUR TIMER FOR A MINIMUM OF 5 MINUTES AND GO THERE!
- ☐ MEDITATION – SET YOUR TIMER FOR A MINIMUM OF 5 MINUTES AND BE PRESENT, IN THE NOW. BREATHE.
- ☐ EXERCISE – DID YOU MOVE AT LEAST 30 MINUTES TODAY?
- ☐ FUEL – EAT 80% NUTRIENT DENSE FOOD THAT ENERGIZES YOU

I WAS MOST GRATEFUL FOR TODAY

Good Evening Gorgeous!

I LOVE TO GIVE. TODAY I GAVE

CHEERS TO ME!!!
LET'S CELEBRATE MY SUCCESSES FOR THE DAY

I AM BRILLIANT
gorgeous
TALENTED AND FABULOUS

I AM GRATEFUL FOR

FUN!!! TODAY FOR FUN I WILL

☐ VISUALIZATION – SET YOUR TIMER FOR A MINIMUM OF 5 MINUTES AND GO THERE!

☐ MEDITATION – SET YOUR TIMER FOR A MINIMUM OF 5 MINUTES AND BE PRESENT, IN THE NOW. BREATHE.

☐ EXERCISE – DID YOU MOVE AT LEAST 30 MINUTES TODAY?

☐ FUEL – EAT 80% NUTRIENT DENSE FOOD THAT ENERGIZES YOU

I WAS MOST GRATEFUL FOR TODAY

Good Evening Gorgeous!

I LOVE TO GIVE. TODAY I GAVE

CHEERS TO ME!!!
LET'S CELEBRATE MY SUCCESSES FOR THE DAY

I AM BRILLIANT
gorgeous
TALENTED AND FABULOUS

GOOD MORNING gorgeous!

I AM GRATEFUL FOR

MY MANTRA *for today!*

FUN!!! TODAY FOR FUN I WILL

- ☐ **VISUALIZATION** – SET YOUR TIMER FOR A MINIMUM OF 5 MINUTES AND GO THERE!
- ☐ **MEDITATION** – SET YOUR TIMER FOR A MINIMUM OF 5 MINUTES AND BE PRESENT, IN THE NOW. BREATHE.
- ☐ **EXERCISE** – DID YOU MOVE AT LEAST 30 MINUTES TODAY?
- ☐ **FUEL** – EAT 80% NUTRIENT DENSE FOOD THAT ENERGIZES YOU

I WAS MOST GRATEFUL FOR TODAY

Good Evening Gorgeous!

I LOVE TO GIVE. TODAY I GAVE

CHEERS TO ME!!!
LET'S CELEBRATE MY SUCCESSES FOR THE DAY

I AM BRILLIANT
gorgeous
TALENTED AND FABULOUS

I AM GRATEFUL FOR

FUN!!! TODAY FOR FUN I WILL

- ☐ **VISUALIZATION** – SET YOUR TIMER FOR A MINIMUM OF 5 MINUTES AND GO THERE!
- ☐ **MEDITATION** – SET YOUR TIMER FOR A MINIMUM OF 5 MINUTES AND BE PRESENT, IN THE NOW. BREATHE.
- ☐ **EXERCISE** – DID YOU MOVE AT LEAST 30 MINUTES TODAY?
- ☐ **FUEL** – EAT 80% NUTRIENT DENSE FOOD THAT ENERGIZES YOU

I WAS MOST GRATEFUL FOR TODAY

Good Evening Gorgeous!

I LOVE TO GIVE. TODAY I GAVE

CHEERS TO ME!!!
LET'S CELEBRATE MY SUCCESSES FOR THE DAY